CHAPTER
29
REVISITED

*The amazing true story of what happens
when a typical American housewife meets Jesus!*

Jean Coleman

ISBN: 1479140007
ISBN-13: 9781479140008
Library of Congress Control Number: 2012915200

CreateSpace, North Charleston, SC

To Jack,
God's special gift to me

TABLE OF CONTENTS

Chapter 1   Thy Servant Hears 1
Chapter 2   The Bread of Life. 13
Chapter 3   Thank You 19
Chapter 4   Into the Wilderness 27
Chapter 5   Into the Fold. 33
Chapter 6   Use Me. 39
Chapter 7   Let Us Witness to Millions 45
Chapter 8   In Everything Give Thanks 53
Chapter 9   And Thy House 59
Chapter 10   Broken Loaves. 65
Chapter 11   Dead and Buried 71
Chapter 12   Silver and Gold 79
Chapter 13   Harvesters into the Field 85
Chapter 14   We Are a Royal Priesthood 93
Chapter 15   Signs and Wonders Following 99
Chapter 16   Who's Speaking? 107
Chapter 17   The Gifts of the Spirit 113
Chapter 18   The Fruit of the Spirit 119
Chapter 19   A Fervent Prayer Answered. 123
Chapter 20   Help My Unbelief 129
Chapter 21   Someday, But Not Now 139
Chapter 22   The Walls Are Tumbling Down 145
Chapter 23   The Prodigals. 151
Chapter 24   Ralph 157
Chapter 25   Life Out of Death. 165
Chapter 26   Yesterday 171
Chapter 27   And Many Other Things 177
Epilogue   The Years That Followed. 179

CHAPTER 1

THY SERVANT HEARS

"God guides thy way if you will let Him come unto you. Heed His word." The words echoed through the silent house and I knew beyond a shadow of a doubt that I had heard the voice of God. The darkness of the room surrounded me, yet a new peace filled the air and I sensed a holy presence.

I pondered the words in my heart, repeating them over and over, trying to comprehend the message that they held for me. *"God guides thy way if you will let Him come unto you. Heed His words."* Strange words spoken in King James English to a twentieth century American housewife. I had always believed that God once spoke to people: to David as he sat in the green pastures playing psalms on his harp, or through visitations by angels to men chosen by God. But surely that had passed away long ago. As far as I was concerned, God seemed to have forgotten us here on earth. Communication between man and God was no more. Yet I knew without any question that God had spoken directly to me.

"God guides thy way" was simple enough to understand. There was no great mystery there. But the second phrase, *"if you will let Him come unto you,"* was very confusing. I had always thought that if I wanted to reach God, I had to go to Him.

Often I had tried to approach God in times of crisis and despair, but the words I heard sounded as though I was the one who was shutting Him out. God seemed to be saying that He wanted to come to me if I would just allow Him entrance.

That night alone in my bedroom, my soul responded to the voice and the calling of the Lord. I whispered, "God, I don't know what You want of me, but I give You my whole life. I can't think of anything more wonderful than to know You and to serve You. If You want me, I give myself to You."

And with a feeling of peace flooding my being, I fell into a deep, restful sleep. I didn't know it, but my life would never be the same again.

In the morning my first conscious thought was of the voice I had heard the night before. The words repeated themselves over and over in my mind. My heart was filled with the knowledge that God Almighty was concerned about me personally and that somehow I fit into His eternal plan.

Up until that time, I knew very little about God. I had some vague, abstract ideas about Him, some basic facts about Jesus, and an interest in the supernatural. Those were not exactly what you would call outstanding qualifications for a person who had just offered herself into His service.

My parents were not churchgoers, but as I was growing up, they were determined that their child would be. Every Sunday morning, rain or shine, I was driven to the nearest Protestant church.

I suppose all kids carry memories of Sunday school days: patent leather shoes and flowery Easter hats, of putting pennies in a church-shaped bank on their birthdays, pins for perfect attendance, and pocket-sized New Testaments for memorizing the books of the Bible.

Other memories too are of a more spiritual nature: the stained glass window of the Good Shepherd carrying a little lamb tenderly in His arms, a certain hymn that seemed to hold a meaning that you couldn't quite grasp, an inner feeling as you sat in church that maybe God was real after all.

But through all the years in Sunday school and church an emptiness prevailed. Many words, many rituals, many prayers, but no reality. No miracles, no demonstrations of the power of God, no answered prayers, no sense of the Lord's presence. Just an emptiness. A semblance of religion with nothing inside. There was no life, just an empty shell.

So like many little girls, I grew up and left my childhood religion behind without ever having experienced the reality of God or even knowing that it was possible to experience the reality. I became inwardly an agnostic, but outwardly a professing Christian.

At sixteen I attended a Baptist church and was very attracted to a handsome young man who was the youth leader. In fact, I was attracted enough to decide to become a Baptist, so I signed up for water baptism. I went into the water a dry sinner and came out a wet sinner, and didn't even know the difference. No one had ever told me that I needed to be saved or even that I was lost. As far as I was concerned, all that was lost was the cute Baptist boy to another girl in the youth group.

In my second year of college, I met another young man on a blind date. His name was Jack and he pursued me vigorously. At the time we had our first date, I was engaged to someone else and really had no business seeing Jack at all, but he was fun to be with and treated me like something very precious. He wouldn't give up, even though I would tell him that I didn't love him. Day after day Jack called to tell me how much he loved me and how happy he would make me if I would marry him. I rejected him time after time. I insulted him and even hung up on him when he called. But still he continued to pursue me and implore me to become his bride.

It was awesome to be loved like that, and as the months wore on and he continued to show his love for me, I found myself learning to love him in return. I saw his patience and goodness and realized that I could spend my life very happily with this persistent suitor.

In life's experiences, God was teaching me a lesson that later I would apply to another Persistent Suitor who would woo me from heaven, desiring me to be His bride.

How blind we mortals be! I was so much like the disciples, walking down the road to Emmaus, who didn't recognize Jesus even though He walked the road with them. Jesus was walking through life with me and I didn't even know who He was or that He was there. But I'm getting ahead of myself.

I finally agreed to marry Jack and we became what you would probably call the typical American family. Jack went to work for the federal government in Virginia, where we lived in a small apartment with our two little girls until we could afford to purchase a home in the Maryland suburbs. We were living the American dream. With the addition of a son and a puppy our family was complete. We didn't have much money, but we were happy together and the years passed uneventfully.

Then in 1964 something very exciting happened. Jack was offered a wonderful opportunity to take a position overseas. It was just too good to turn down. So we rented our house, packed up our belongings and moved to Australia where we were attached to the consulate in Melbourne for four years. We moved with the diplomatic set in a round of cocktail parties, fancy dinners and social events.

My life was transformed and I loved every minute of my time there. I had found my identity. No longer just another housewife, I knew who I was. In a sense, I was a representative of the United States of America serving as an ambassador of sorts. I was eager to make a good impression upon all the Australians that we met, knowing that they were recognizing me as an American and judging my country by my actions. We made many Australian friends while we were there, but felt a real warmth toward the other Americans because of our common bond.

Once again God was teaching me spiritual lessons from my life's experiences because it would not be too long until I was once again a stranger in a foreign land. Soon I would be "Christ's ambassador," representing the kingdom of God and the King of kings and Lord of lords.

All that was hidden from me at the time. God was far from my thoughts in Australia. The entire time we were living there, we never spent a Sunday morning in church. Sundays were made for sleeping, for picnics and for doing our own thing. Those were very busy days with no time left over for God. I thought I was living life to the fullest.

I must admit that sometimes at night as I lay in bed, my thoughts would turn to the Lord. When I couldn't sleep, I would wonder if I was lying there awake because I had forgotten to say my prayers. Some childhood habits stay with a person for a long time and I had been taught to always say my prayers before going to sleep.

Questions would often run through my mind as I waited for sleep to come. Was there really a God? Where was God? Who was God? Why had I been born? What was the meaning of life? What would happen to me when I died? There were many questions, but never any answers.

Then my four magic years in Australia came to an end and I was back home again in Maryland. After our exciting time in Australia, life in the suburbs was very dull. We were once again living in our old house with each piece of furniture sitting in the same exact place it had been before. It was like we had never been away. Four years of my life had vanished.

I fought depression and discouragement. I was bored and unhappy and began having stomach aches and backaches. The monotonous routine of keeping house and driving kids from place to place stretched before me endlessly. Life held no meaning, no purpose.

I began to take pep pills in the morning followed by numerous cups of coffee throughout the day. Around five o'clock the pep pills would wear off and I would take a tranquilizer, washed down with a drink or two before dinner to deaden the boredom of the evening. I was smoking over two packs of cigarettes a day. Life didn't seem worth living.

Tears came easily and for no reason. One night after dinner, I was standing at the sink washing the dishes and I began to cry. Jack walked into the kitchen and found me sobbing.

"What's the matter with you?" he asked with compassion putting his arms around me.

I didn't know how to answer his question. I had everything that a woman could possibly want: a loving husband, three nice, healthy children, a beautiful home, two cars and lots of friends. I should have been happy and content, but there was an emptiness in my life that I couldn't even explain.

According to statistics, we had it made. We had achieved success. Yet although I had everything, inside I felt like I had nothing. It seemed like there had to be more to life than what I was experiencing. Was this what life was all about? One is born, lives and dies. Why? What is the meaning of it all? I felt empty and alone.

And then in May of 1970, Jack had a major heart attack. I had often read in magazines about men having heart attacks, but Jack was still a young man and it certainly wasn't something that I was expecting at his age. How could this possibly be happening to us?

As I sat in the emergency room waiting for the doctor's report, I had never felt so alone in my life. There was nothing I could do but pray, and in faith I reached out to the Lord for His help.

"Dear God, please don't let this be a heart attack," I pleaded. "Please let Jack be all right. Do something, Lord. Don't let him die. Help me!"

When the doctor appeared, he wasn't the bearer of good news. The diagnosis had been confirmed. It was a major heart attack and there had been some permanent damage to Jack's heart.

Suddenly life became a precious commodity, something to be treasured. The drive of ambition with the expectation of promotions, salary increases and getting ahead wasn't important anymore. All that mattered was that I loved Jack and that he was alive.

Through the years our love had become somewhat lukewarm. We had become more involved with raising kids, making money and moving ahead than in our relationship with one another. But now my priorities were put in order and love for Jack became first and foremost. For the first time in years, Jack came before Jean as my major concern. I wondered how much longer I was going to have him alive. Each day was one for which to be thankful . Tests showed that the heart damage was minor, but Jack's recovery was a slow process. He spent three and a half weeks in the hospital and then another six and a half weeks at home regaining his strength.

Living with a man who has had a heart attack is like living with a time bomb. You find yourself wondering when it is going to go off. I clucked over Jack like a mother hen: "Don't lift this. Don't do that. Be careful that you don't go up the stairs too fast." I was his caregiver and his guardian, watching his diet and his every move.

Finally Jack was told he was well enough to return to work. The memory of standing at the front door watching him drive off to his office alone will always stay with me. He was no longer in my care and under my watchful eye.

To an unknown God I prayed, "You're going to have to watch over Jack now. I'm not with him and there's nothing that I can do about his heart. I just have to give Jack to You and trust that You will take care of him."

As time passed, I watched Jack grow strong and healthy again. The doctor nodded his approval over Jack's progress and my constant anxiety faded into just occasional bouts of worry. A strong sense of love and the wonder of the gift of life remained implanted in my heart Also remaining was a need for the sense of security I had experienced when I had placed Jack into God's hands.

Everything was going along fine until I developed insomnia. I began to lie in bed for hours unable to sleep. Night was a time that I dreaded. I would lie awake in the darkness mulling over the trials of the day, worrying about money, the kids' activities and Jack's heart. I made elaborate lists in my mind as I waited for sleep to come: shopping lists, lists of things to do around the house, lists of clothes the children would need for school in the fall. Still sleep wouldn't come. It was like my mind was in overdrive.

Finally when all the worries and problems had been reviewed, I would turn my thoughts toward God. I began to ponder the Lord's Prayer that I had said religiously since I was a child. Phrase by phrase I attempted to figure out just what I was saying when I repeated the memorized words.

"Our Father" seemed like an unusual way to start the prayer. How could I call a perfect stranger my father? God may have been Jesus' father, but He certainly wasn't mine. I didn't even know for sure that God existed. A father is someone who is related to you. He's someone you love and to whom you feel close. How could I possibly begin my prayer by calling God my father when I didn't even know Him?

"Which art in heaven." Where was heaven? I didn't know, but I thought that it was probably somewhere up in the sky. I

8

hoped that when I died, I would go there, but I really wasn't sure whether I would or not. Heaven remained a great unsolved mystery in my mind.

Phrase by phrase I would go through this mystery prayer that I had prayed nightly since I was a child. It simply made no sense. The only part I really understood was *"Give us this day our daily bread."* I certainly could understand praying for daily bread considering the price I was paying for groceries to feed our hungry family.

"Forgive us our debts." Debts meant sins. When I was asking God to forgive my debts, I was asking Him to forgive my sins. I knew that much. Had I committed any sins recently? None that I could really remember. Not any major sins anyway. I was a good person and certainly not a sinner.

I didn't realize at the time that for years I had only been "saying" the Lord's Prayer, instead of "praying" the Lord's Prayer. Little did I know the deep work that the Lord was doing in my heart as I pondered these things during my sleepless nights.

There were many more spiritual questions that I would ask myself as I lay there waiting for morning to come. Night thoughts and night questions, hour after hour, running through my mind. How did I come to be? What was the purpose of my life? Why was man created?

I pondered for hours the fact that people are living on earth and that everything they need for their existence has been provided. What an amazing thing. It was almost too amazing to be called a coincidence.

I thought about what a complex being I am, a person capable of thinking, loving, growing, planning, reproducing. Could all that be the result of an accident of nature? Or is man someone created by an all-knowing Creator, who was aware of man's needs and provided everything for him?

The more I thought about these things, the more I became convinced that mankind has a Creator. I had always believed in evolution, the big bang theory, but slowly my thinking began to change. I realized that I couldn't have just happened by chance or by the splitting of a few atoms. I had a Creator and that Creator was God. My first few baby steps had been taken toward an encounter with the living God.

There were other questions to be answered. What about Jesus? I thought a lot about Him too. Who was Jesus? What did I believe about Jesus Christ? On my bed I recalled all I had learned about Jesus in Sunday School and church over the years.

Did I believe that Jesus had been born of a virgin? Definitely yes. Did I believe that He did mighty miracles as He walked on earth? Again, definitely yes. I believed that Jesus had healed the sick and made blind eyes to see and deaf ears to hear. Yes, I believed in the miracles of Jesus.

I also believed that Jesus died on the cross and that He had been buried in a tomb for three days and three nights. I didn't doubt for a moment that He rose from the dead and was seen by many after His resurrection. I wasn't sure what had happened to Jesus after He was raised from the dead, but I did know that He was in heaven with God. We used to say in church every Sunday that He was "seated at the right hand of the Father." I had the facts and I believed them. I believed them in my mind, but not in my heart.

Then there was the big question. Did I believe that Jesus was the Son of God? I thought deeply about that. I had never known of anyone else like Jesus. He was certainly different from any other man who had walked the earth. Surely He must have been the Son of God.

This was another step in the right direction toward God. *"He that comes to God must believe that He is"* (Hebrews 11:6). If I was acknowledging Jesus as the Son of God, then I was also saying that God is His Father. I was confessing that God exists. It was a very big step. There is a God and Jesus is God's Son. Now I knew the truth not only in my head, but also in my heart.

10

Through those long nights of sleeplessness, I explored the simple truths of God and moved closer to the day when my heart was prepared to receive Him as <u>my</u> God.

January 8th, 1972 was a normal Saturday. Jack and I had worked hard all day and into the evening laying carpeting in the family room in our basement. There was no hint, no indication, that this day would mark the beginning of a new life in the presence of God. There was nothing to set the day apart. Only God knew that what was going to happen would turn my world upside down and inside out and launch me on the greatest adventure that anyone can possibly undertake. I was about to begin my life as a follower of Jesus Christ.

That January night was the night that I heard the voice of God speaking to me. *"God guides thy way if you will let Him come unto you. Heed His word."*

CHAPTER 2

THE BREAD OF LIFE

Hearing the voice of God doesn't mean that you have been handed a one-way ticket to heaven. It only means that you have taken the first step on the road of faith that is going to be rough and crooked and up and down. Hearing the voice of God for the first time often brings confusion and conviction.

It also brings doubt. I guess the first reaction as I faced the new day was, "Did this really happen to me?" Perhaps I dreamed it, or maybe it was just a wild thought that floated through my imagination. I just couldn't acknowledge the words that I had heard as my words. They didn't say what I would say. They were contrary to what I believed.

Deep down in my heart, I knew that the words were real. I had heard the call of God. God was real and He had spoken to me. God Almighty had actually spoken to me. In a world of three billion people, God had somehow called to me, a housewife in a small town in Maryland. Why? I didn't know the answer to that question yet, but more than anything else, I wanted to find out why the Lord would speak to me.

I thought about God all day and said the words over and over to myself, puzzling over the fact that He wanted to "come unto me." There was a sense of unreality throughout the entire day.

It was as though I had been taken back in time. I tried to relate the knowledge that God had spoken to me to the experiences others had in the past. I knew that the Lord had spoken to people in the Old Testament, but I couldn't recall ever hearing of any modern day communication from Him. As far as I knew, God had stopped talking to anyone.

In the afternoon I put up the ironing board in the bedroom, and as I ironed, I continued to go over in my mind what had happened to me. And then clearly I again heard the voice of God, *"Eat of the Bread of Life."*

Strange words to hear as I was doing the ironing. Words of mystery spoken in a gentle voice, *"Eat of the Bread of Life."*

What was the Bread of Life? I had no idea.

"What are You saying to me, God?" I asked. "I don't understand what You're trying to tell me." Confusion closed in upon me. Could I be losing my mind? People who hear voices are locked up in mental hospitals. What was happening to me?

Suddenly there was a strong urge within me. There were no words, just the sudden need to find a Bible. I quickly left the ironing board and went into the kitchen to get a flashlight. For our fifth anniversary thirteen years before, Jack's mother had sent us a Bible. It was up in the attic still in the box, unopened except to read the inscription on the flyleaf. I rushed into the attic and began a frantic search through boxes and cartons looking for the Bible which had become terribly important to locate.

I had never given much thought to the Bible. As a teenager I had made resolutions several times to read a chapter every day. I usually made it through four or five chapters of Genesis and then became discouraged or bored. But now finding the Bible had almost become a matter of life or death.

And then, there it was in the bottom of a box way back in the corner of the attic. I spent the rest of the afternoon looking through it, trying to find something about the Bread of Life. It was like looking for a needle in a haystack. I didn't even know for sure that those words were in the Bible, but I had a feeling that what I was searching for could be found in this black leather book.

Jack came home from work and I shared with him my experience of the night before, as well as the words that I had heard spoken that afternoon. I expected him to be really enthusiastic and excited over my revelation, but Jack hardly paid any attention at all. He simply informed me that he didn't know anything about any Bread of Life, and then asked when dinner would be ready.

All evening long I continued to look through the pages of the Bible looking for the key to God's reason for speaking to me. Page by page I continued my search. I felt somehow that my answer was in the New Testament, perhaps in Matthew, Mark, Luke or John. Hours passed as I skimmed over the many chapters. Jack went to bed and still I continued to turn the pages one by one.

And then I saw it leaping up at me from the page. In John 6:35 I read these words, *"Jesus said unto them, I am the Bread of Life: he that comes to Me shall never hunger and he that believes on Me shall never thirst."*

My heart beat wildly within me. God had confirmed His word. The words spoken to me were right there in the Bible. Words unknown to me, with no meaning to me, were contained in the sacred pages of His word.

It was true! It was real! God had actually spoken to me! I knew now without a doubt that I had heard the voice of God. God was alive! He was real! God had spoken to me!

I knew how excited Jack would be, so I ran into the bedroom shouting, "Jack, wake up! You're never going to believe this. Look at this in the Bible."

I turned on the light and handed him his glasses. Jack rolled over and looked at the words I was pointing out in the Bible. "Uh-huh," he muttered and closed his eyes again.

"Honey, look at this!" I pleaded. "You see it really was God speaking to me. Look what it says right here. *"Jesus said, I am the Bread of Life."* God was talking to me about Jesus. Can't you see? It's all real. God really did speak to me. Isn't it wonderful?"

But Jack had already gone back to sleep.

I put on my pajamas and got into bed, but I didn't sleep. My heart was filled to overflowing. I was awed by the revelation that God still spoke to people and that He had spoken to me. The unbelievable had become believable. I finally drifted off to sleep talking to the Lord, saying over and over, "Thank You, God. Thank You, God."

The following day, joy welled up in my heart. I felt like I was walking ten feet off the ground. I read John chapter six over and over trying to find out what Jesus meant when He said that He was the Bread of Life. What He was trying to convey escaped me entirely and frustration began to set in. There was no doubt that I needed some help in my search for understanding, but where could I find it?

We were members of the local Presbyterian church and attended on Easter and sometimes at Christmas time. Our pledge to the church was the generous sum of one dollar weekly. Every three months they would send us an offering statement and I would mail them a check. The minister had made a few calls when Jack had his heart attack, but he was really a stranger to me.

Somehow I just didn't see how I could call the minister on the phone and say, "Remember me? I'm a member of your church and two nights ago God spoke to me. Can you help me understand what He was saying?"

That really seemed like it would be a bit too much. Yet in my heart remained the hunger to learn the meaning of God's special message to me. I had to find out what the Bread of Life signified.

Then I had an idea. Perhaps somewhere on Sunday morning a sermon was going to be preached on this passage and I could go to the church to hear it. So I spread out the local newspaper before me and skimmed the advertisements on the religious page seeking a clue somewhere. There was nothing about the Bread of Life that I could see. Where did one go to learn about this bread?

Suddenly I saw it! The name of the minister at the Methodist church in town was named Reverend Baker. Of course. If you wanted to know about bread, you would ask a baker.

On an impulse, I went to the phone and dialed the number listed beside his name. "Lord," I prayed, "if you want me to talk to this minister, please have him answer the phone."

The phone rang three times and then came the answer, "First Methodist Church. Reverend Baker speaking."

I took a deep breath and plunged in. "You don't know me, but I have a very important question and I need to have the answer. I thought perhaps you could help me."

Reverend Baker didn't even ask my name, but merely replied, "I'll certainly do what I can. What's the question?"

My heart was pounding within me. "What did Jesus mean when He said, I am the Bread of Life?"

There was a pause before the answer came. "Jesus was saying that He is the spiritual food that every man must have if his spirit is to grow in wisdom and truth."

A light went on in my being! Illumination shone forth in the darkness of my soul. Of course, it was all so clear now. Without food my body would become weak, undernourished and eventually it would die. I had to eat to stay alive and healthy.

Spiritually it was the same principle. My spirit could not grow and live without spiritual food. Jesus was the food God had provided for my spirit to feed upon. Without Jesus I could not have spiritual life.

I nearly shouted into the phone. "Oh, thank you. That's just the right answer I needed to hear. I can never tell you how much this means to me."

Reverend Baker answered simply, "I'm glad I could be of help. If you have any more questions, be sure to call me again."

I hung up the phone and sent up a prayer of thanksgiving to God. "Thank You, Lord. Thank You so very much."

I had my answer. Jesus was the Bread of Life my spirit needed. I wasn't sure how to find Jesus or how to feed upon Him when I did. But I did know that without Jesus, I was spiritually dead. And I also knew that I wanted spiritual life. I needed Jesus.

CHAPTER 3

THANK YOU

Every day I walked in the presence of God. I would often hear the Lord speak to me in a still, small voice simply saying my name over and over. Or He would say something like, *"Walk with Me"* or perhaps the words, *"I am with you."* I was conscious of the nearness of God twenty-four hours a day. There became an awareness that not only was God with me, but that He was also within me. His voice was no longer audible only through my outer ear, but through my inner spiritual ear as well.

There was also the realization that God knew what was going on inside of me as well as on the outside. It was like He knew my every thought. Often when I would entertain a wrong thought, I would hear a gentle rebuke from within. A growing sense of conviction came upon me. It was as though someone was shining a giant searchlight inside of me and looking into all the dirty corners of my mind. For the first time I became acutely aware of many things that were hidden within me, ugly defiling things. On the inside, I was an unholy mess.

My thoughts made me want to dig a hole and climb into it. My reactions to people and situations made me despair. I suddenly started seeing myself as God saw me and I was ashamed.

I started reading the New Testament in the Bible and it didn't take me too long to get to Matthew 5:21-22 and these words, *"You have heard it said by them of old, thou shalt not kill and whosoever shall kill shall be in danger of the judgment. But I say unto you, that whosoever is angry with his brother without a cause shall be in danger of the judgment."* Sobering words indeed.

I had never really thought of myself as a sinner. I was aware of the ten commandments and considered myself a pretty good commandment keeper. *"Thou shalt not kill."* I had never killed anyone, so obviously I had scored ten points in the record book of heaven for keeping that commandment perfectly.

"Thou shalt not commit adultery." I loved Jack and had been faithful to him over the years. Definitely I would be awarded another ten points on that commandment.

"Honor thy father and mother." I presented myself with another gold star for that one. I loved my parents, wrote to them once a week and called them on the phone regularly. I certainly honored them.

"Thou shalt not steal." Another plus ten points in the Lord's record book. Even as a child, I didn't steal. I think I was always afraid of getting caught. I may have cheated in school, but I wasn't a thief.

Of course, there were a few commandments that I had slipped up on a little. I did take the Lord's name in vain, but then so did everyone else. And the same was true of coveting and telling lies. These seemingly unimportant little things may have brought my commandment-keeping score down a little, but certainly I had achieved a passing grade. I was a good person with as much of a chance of getting into heaven as anyone else.

Maybe I had done a few bad things in my lifetime. There were some minor slipups along the path of life, but nothing serious. And I had done more than enough good things to offset the bad. I had cooked meals for sick friends and invited an old man to have Christmas dinner with us once. I loved animals, helped out the neighbors when they had problems and had even given blood to the Red Cross. The good would cancel out the bad.

However, the way Jesus interpreted the commandments was certainly different from the way I did. Reading Matthew, I learned that Jesus considered anger to be as bad as murder. That put a whole different slant on things because I was an angry person. I was angry at my husband, my kids, the dog for barking, and my neighbor for running his lawn mower before ten o'clock on Saturday mornings. If I dropped a dish on the floor, I was even angry with the dish and shouted a few swear words at it. There was no doubt that I was filled with anger.

Jesus also wrote His thoughts on adultery. *"Ye have heard it said by them of old, thou shall not commit adultery. But I say unto you that whosoever looks on a woman to lust after her has committed adultery with her already in his heart" (Matthew 5:27-28).*

That made me pause for thought. Certainly I had lusted in my heart over the years. I had read dirty books that I had to hide when the children came into the room and even attended X-rated movies at the Drive-In. There was no way that I could say I had never lusted.

As I read the Bible, I became convicted of just how sinful I really was. In Romans 6:29, I read that *"the wages of sin is death."* My sin had been exposed and I didn't know what to do about it. I felt dirty and unclean, deserving of death. The light was shining into my life and everything hidden was being exposed.

My joy of being in the presence of God quickly diminished. I tried to flee from the Lord, to hide myself from Him, but He was always there. I was a sinner in the presence of God and there was no place to hide.

I would take a shower and the presence of the Lord was so real in the bathroom that I would try to cover myself with the washcloth so that He wouldn't see my nakedness. My reaction was the same as that of Adam and Eve after they had sinned in the garden of Eden. They tried to hide from God's presence and attempted to cover themselves with fig leaves. But I couldn't hide from God. There was no way to cover up my sinfulness. It was impossible. The Lord was everywhere that I went, shining the searchlight of the spirit into my heart and soul, and bringing into view more and more of my sins from the past and present. The harder I tried to avoid sin, the stronger the pull of it seemed to become.

I was a sinner and I knew it. I was a disgrace to God and to myself. I tried to mend my ways, change my thoughts, alter my reactions, clean myself up, but I couldn't. The harder I tried, the worse it all became. I had days when I wondered if I was losing my mind. My wonderful experience with God had turned into a nightmare from which I couldn't awake.

Finally one day in complete desperation, I fell to my knees and cried out, "Oh God, what am I going to do?"

Once again I heard the audible voice of God speaking very clearly to me. *"Remember, Jesus Christ died for your sins."*

Praise God! I understood at last. Hundreds of times before I had heard those same words. I had heard them in Sunday School, in church, on television and even read them on tracts that people had pressed into my hand. But now I understood the meaning of the words. Jesus Christ died for me! Not only for some nameless people two thousand years ago, but Jesus had died for me personally. Jesus took the punishment that I deserved for my sin. He had set me free from my sin.

In my mind's eye, I approached Jesus on the cross. In my hands I held a book, and in the book were written down all the sins that I had ever committed in my thirty-six years of life. As I stood at the foot of the cross, the blood of Jesus flowed down upon the pages of the book. As I watched, the pages miraculously turned white. The long list of sins vanished and my sins were washed away in the precious blood of God's own Son. The pages were free from all condemnation. The blood of Jesus had acted upon them like ink eradicator. and my sins were gone, never to return.

I had been given a new start and a new beginning.

"Jesus Christ, the same yesterday and today and forever" (Heb.13:8). Time has no meaning for God and as Jesus hung on the cross for the men of yesteryear, He is still there by faith for all those who will come today for redemption. Jesus is the One who opens the door of heaven to those who believe in Him as Savior and Lord.

I was born again and tears of relief and joy flowed from me. For the first time as a child of God, I lifted my hands to heaven and said, "Thank You, Father." No longer a stranger, God had become my Heavenly Father.

Jesus had become my Savior. My sins had been washed away and I entered into the presence of God without guilt, without sin, without fear and without condemnation. I was right with God and I knew it. Jesus had given me eternal life and I was no longer under a death penalty. God was now my Father and I loved Him with a love that could not be described.

Jesus had stepped out of the Bible and became a Living Person to be worshiped and adored throughout eternity. A miracle had taken place in my life. All I could do was say, "Thank You, Lord. Thank You so very much!"

Each morning as I awoke my first thought was, "I am saved. I'm a child of God. God is with me. I love Him and life is wonderful."

I sang praises to God all day long. I knew only a few songs of worship, but the ones I knew I sang over and over. My favorite song was "Joyful, Joyful, We Adore Thee," and I sang it maybe five hundred times a day. Even our parrot learned to sing along with me. Joy filled my heart and flooded my soul. I talked to the Lord constantly and walked in His presence.

I couldn't get enough of the Bible. Jesus had become my Heavenly Bridegroom and I wanted to learn all I could about this One with whom I was going to spend my eternal life. I became the most efficient housewife in the world. All my daily chores were completed by nine o'clock in the morning and then I was free to devote myself for the rest of the day to the study of God's word. My soul fed upon the Bread of Life and I grew day by day in the things of the Lord.

I read about the disciples who followed Jesus, and it wasn't too long before I could identify with them. The disciples in the Bible were so much like me, sometimes too sure of themselves and at other times not sure enough. They always seemed to be saying the wrong thing or doing the wrong thing, continually disappointing Jesus with their unbelief.

It was like the disciples were enrolled in the school of the spirit. I read how Jesus had sent them forth to cast out demons, heal the sick and to spread the Gospel. I knew that the Lord wanted me to be doing those same things, but I just didn't know how. I recognized that I was called to be a disciple, but I was far from being the disciple Jesus wanted me to be.

I longed to tell people about my wonderful experience and how Jesus had saved me, but I just couldn't get the words out of my mouth because of nervousness and fear. I actually invited my neighbor over to the house for coffee five days in a row, and although we talked for hours, I never had enough courage to tell her about Jesus. I wanted to, but I just couldn't.

Then one day I started reading the Book of Acts and found that a marvelous thing had happened to the disciples. They stopped blundering around and started winning souls to Jesus. On the day of Pentecost they led three thousand souls to the Lord. People were healed and demons were cast out. The disciples seemed to be no longer concerned about what people thought of them. They had been given power to witness.

The disciples had what I wanted and needed. They had received power. As far as I could tell from reading the scriptures, they had been baptized in the Holy Spirit. Jesus had sent the Holy Spirit to them and the disciples had been filled and empowered to serve the Lord.

So on March 9th, 1972, I knelt at the side of my bed, lifted my hands toward heaven and said simply, "Jesus, give me the same power that You gave the disciples on the day of Pentecost. Here I am, Lord. Fill me."

Immediately Jesus poured out the Holy Spirit upon me. It was as though I was hit with a lightning bolt. Wave after wave of power flowed through me as I received the gift of the Holy Spirit and accepted the infilling from on high. Words of love to the Lord flowed forth from my mouth as I praised Him and felt His love well up inside of me. I lost track of time as I worshipped Jesus as Savior, Lord, and as Baptizer in the Holy Spirit.

In my sheltered (or practically non-existent) religious background, I had never heard of Pentecostals, Charismatics or Spirit-filled people. I discovered Pentecost in the Bible and claimed it for myself from the promise in God's word. When I got off of my knees that day in March, I knew that the power of God flowed through me and that I was going to be His witness to the uttermost parts of the earth. I had been called and equipped to be a servant of Almighty God.

That evening the minister from the Baptist church in town just happened to stop by our house to make a call. Jack and I had attended his church the previous week and filled out a visitor's card giving our name and address. I was so excited when this pastor showed up at our door because I was just waiting for an opportunity to witness to someone about what Jesus had done for me that afternoon.

He was obviously a born again man, but I didn't care. I told him all about hearing the voice of God and receiving Jesus as my Savior. I also told him how I had been baptized in the Holy Spirit and even offered to pray for him that he might also receive this powerful gift from God.

After listening to my testimony for about thirty minutes, the Baptist preacher grabbed his hat and coat and nearly fled from our house. He didn't even stay long enough to allow me to pray with him to receive the Holy Spirit.

With great joy, I had entered into the Spirit-filled life and set about living my own chapter of the book of Acts.

CHAPTER 4

INTO THE WILDERNESS

I wish I could say that from that day on life was a bed of roses, but it wasn't like that at all. What happened to Jesus after He was baptized by John and the Holy Spirit descended upon Him? The Bible states that He was led by the Spirit into the wilderness to be tempted by the devil. And I too was led into the wilderness.

My heart was filled with joy as I moved into this new relationship with the Lord, and I little expected the trials and tribulations that awaited me. I was a new creature in Christ Jesus and it never occurred to me that some people wouldn't be happy with the "new Jean" who had come into being.

God was getting ready to fashion me into the vessel that He desired to use to accomplish His will. The Potter had His hands upon the clay, and now that the water of the Spirit had been added, the Lord was ready to start molding and shaping me into a woman who could be used for His glory.

Three days after I received the baptism of the Spirit, God again spoke to my heart. We had spent the evening with friends and I had just gotten into bed for the night when I heard His voice.

"Jean, do you love Me?"

"Lord, You know that I love You."

"Then I want you to quit smoking."

"Lord, I can't quit smoking. I've tried, but You know that I smoke nearly three packs every day. I just can't quit smoking."

"Jean, do you love Me?"

"Lord, You know that I love You, but I just can't do it."

"I am with you and I will help you. I will give you the strength. When you want a cigarette, put a prayer on your lips instead. Your body is My temple and it is not to be defiled."

"Lord, I love You."

The next morning I woke up with the memory of the previous night's conversation with the Lord in my mind. It was Sunday, so by eight o'clock I was at the Methodist church for their early service. At nine-thirty I quickly drove over to the Presbyterian church to attend Sunday School and then remained for the church service at eleven o'clock.

By the time I returned home a little after noon, I still hadn't smoked a cigarette and I knew that I wasn't ever going to smoke again. I had claimed another promise from the Bible: *"I can do all things through Christ who strengthens me"* (Philippians 4:13).

Five o'clock found me in the kitchen on my knees in constant prayer while I was trying to fix dinner for the family. But I knew that I had the victory. And in two days it was all over. I was an ex-smoker and the Holy Spirit no longer dwelt in a smoke-filled temple.

A Spirit-filled person, who is empowered to witness, is certainly going to need someone with whom the good news can be shared. Guess who was the most convenient? Jack, of course!

Poor Jack! He got up in the morning to the sound of my voice singing the praises of God as I prepared his breakfast. Then he sat patiently at the table as I prayed, offering thanks to the Lord for the food, for Jesus, for salvation, for my family and on and on and on.

When Jack came home from work, I greeted him at the door with a kiss and then proceeded to tell him about all the wonderful things I had read in the Bible during the day.

I gave my husband a daily diet of Jesus. He didn't want to eat the spiritual food I was providing, but I shoved it down his throat anyway. It was like trying to feed strained carrots to a baby who doesn't want strained carrots. Eventually the baby will spit the carrots out or push the bowl away. Even worse, the child may become so turned off to carrots that he will never eat them again. This is what was happening to Jack. I was force-feeding him and getting nowhere at all.

Jack also didn't care for some of my new habits, like reading the Bible, praying and singing hymns. "All you want to do now," he told me, "is to read the Bible. I'm tired of seeing you with the Bible in your hand all the time."

"Honey, what does it matter to you whether I read the Bible or a sexy novel?" Stony silence from Jack.

"Please don't ask me to go to the movie with you to see that R-rated picture tonight." More silence from Jack.

"But why should I have a drink before dinner when I don't need or want a drink before dinner? I don't take an aspirin when I don't have a headache." Again, silence from Jack.

My husband grew more and more sullen. Our happy marriage turned sour as Jack tried to become acquainted with this new woman who was now his wife.

"I don't even like you anymore," he would tell me. "If I met you today, I wouldn't even ask you out on a date. We just don't have anything in common. I don't like anything about you. You aren't any fun at all."

Often I would go alone into the bedroom and kneel beside the bed to pray for Jack. "Forgive him, Father. Jack's in darkness and he just doesn't understand everything that is happening. Draw him to You, Lord. I love him and I know that You love him even more than I do. Please save him. Do whatever it takes to bring Jack into the kingdom."

In the Bible I had found a wonderful promise. In Acts chapter 16:31 were recorded these words, *"Believe on the Lord Jesus Christ and you will be saved and your entire household."* I knew in my heart that Jack was going to meet the Lord. It was just taking a lot longer than I had anticipated.

The Lord was doing a mighty work in Jack and things seemed to get worse and worse as Jack fought against the conviction of the Holy Spirit. I had stopped preaching to Jack and just started loving him. Instead of witnessing to him in words, I had started being a witness through my life. But the love and compassion I was exhibiting toward him just seemed to make the situation worse.

Finally came the evening when Jack announced, "Jean, I don't think that I can continue on with this marriage any more. You've become a real religious fanatic and I can't stand to be around you."

My heart was broken and I didn't even know how to reply. "Jack, I love you and I want you to be happy. What do I need to do to make you happy? Tell me what you want me to do."

He looked at me with disgust. "I don't even know. Just leave me alone." And Jack turned and walked away.

I went out into the kitchen and leaned against the refrigerator, feeling the tears running down my cheeks. All I could do was pray.

"Lord, I love Jack, but I'm not turning back. Even if this costs me my marriage, I'm not turning back. I can't live the way I used to live or be the person I used to be. I'm not turning back."

My decision had been made and I believe that in that declaration I answered the call to follow Jesus as a disciple. I was willing to forsake all. Yet within me there was an inner peace. I knew in my heart that I was not going to lose Jack and that God was in control of the whole situation.

Through my mind flashed the story of Abraham and Isaac. Abraham thought that he was going to have to sacrifice his son and was prepared to trust the Lord with the life of his precious child. But just when it looked as though everything was lost, the Lord interceded and Abraham didn't have to give up his son after all. The important thing is that he was willing to make the sacrifice if that was what God required of him.

And through my experience, God revealed to me that it is our willingness to sacrifice that really counts with Him. I had demonstrated to the Lord that I was willing to lay my marriage upon the altar. He knew my heart and that I would follow Him no matter what the cost

Within my innermost being, I knew that God had given Jack back to me and that He would restore our marriage. All I had to do was trust the Lord and give Him time to work the power of His mercy and saving grace in Jack's life.

So I just kept on loving Jack with the love of the Lord. And slowly I saw the miracle begin to unfold. First I noticed a little stem pushing up through the hard ground of Jack's heart. Then there were a few leaves that began to unfurl and the evidence of buds beginning to form. I knew that it wouldn't be too long until Jack would burst into bloom as the light of the Son continued to shine on him through me.

I had learned a great truth. Love never fails.

CHAPTER 5

INTO THE FOLD

It is hard to be a Spirit-filled Christian when you think that you are the only Spirit-filled Christian in the world. I wandered from church to church trying to locate "my people" somewhere. I frightened the Presbyterians and the Methodists, and even the Baptists seemed to be somewhat leery of my enthusiasm and excitement over knowing Jesus.

I had visited our minister at the Presbyterian church, and he had listened patiently to the story of my conversion. However, he then proceeded to warn me not to come on too strongly with my husband about Jesus because I would wreck my marriage.

I had also made an appointment to meet personally with Reverend Baker at the Methodist church. Dr. Baker was the pastor who had told me on the phone about how the Bread of Life was spiritual food. But when I shared with him about hearing God's voice and being born again, he informed me that I must have been seeking a religious experience and only imagined everything that had happened.

"You have to be realistic," he advised me. "You need to remember that your imagination can play some really funny tricks on you."

It was a real shock when I realized that there are many ministers who have never met Jesus personally. Like the Pharisees of old, they embrace *"a form of godliness, but deny its power"* (II Timothy 3:5). I was really disillusioned by some of the men of the cloth who tried to turn me away from the path of faith.

As time passed, I met a number of people in various churches who really knew and loved Jesus, however none of them seemed to know anything about the second experience that I had received. My boldness seemed to turn off many people in the churches and I couldn't understand their lack of passion for the gospel. Many seemed embarrassed when I spoke about my love for Jesus and even tried to avoid talking with me on Sunday mornings.

Loneliness would come upon me at times and I would pray, "Lord, where are the other people who know You and hear Your voice?"

I knew that I was certainly not the only one who had been called by God and chosen to serve Him. The Lord is reaching out to anyone who will believe and put their trust in Him. But I had also come to understand that not everyone has the ears to hear. Over and over, I had read these words in the Bible, *"He who has the ears to hear, let him hear"* (Matthew 13:9).

From January until September, I walked a lonely path. I rejoiced in the presence of God but also longed for human fellowship. I continued to look for someone to talk with concerning spiritual things, and also sought a church where I could be spiritually fed and used by God.

Of course, the Lord was always with me and ministered to me daily from the word. I often felt like He had separated me from other believers so that I would spend time alone with Him.

As the months passed, it became obvious that the Lord had called me to be a Bible teacher. He directed my studies in a firm manner through an inner guidance and the still small voice.

"Too much is read into the Bible and not enough out," God informed me one morning. *"Don't read in. Read what the word says and then believe it without question."*

The Lord also taught me obedience and discipline in the study of the word. I was a speed- reader and was able to read an entire 350-page novel in an evening. But God had other ideas when it came to reading the Bible. His instructions were very specific.

"Starting in the Gospel of Matthew, you may read one chapter a day. Only one chapter. Remember, just one chapter."

I would plead with the Lord. "One chapter a day isn't nearly enough. One chapter is like reading nothing. How can I read just one chapter of the Bible a day?"

"Read that chapter a hundred times and then you will really know and understand what it says. Read your chapter from many different versions."

Discipline and more discipline.

"I've finished reading Matthew, Mark, Luke and John. Now what?"

"Read them over again. You can never read the four gospels too many times. Hide the word in your heart."

I studied and read my textbook, the Bible, for hours at a time. My teacher was the Holy Spirit who brought the word to life. Line upon line and precept upon precept it all began to come together. I found that not only was Jesus the center of the New Testament, but that He was also found in the Old Testament through shadows and types.

I grew in the knowledge of the word, and in September I was invited to teach an adult Sunday school class in the local Presbyterian church that we attended. I had been given the opportunity to share the word of God in a church that badly needed to hear it. The Lord was beginning to open doors and to use me.

Yet I was still lonely and often felt rejected by everyone. I was a misfit in the churches and persecuted by my husband and children. My mother suggested that I see a psychiatrist. My neighbors no longer invited me over for coffee. I continued to pray, "Lord, where are my people?"

Then one day in October, there was a knock on the front door. I opened it to find two young men standing there wearing white shirts and neckties. They had short haircuts and each carried a Bible under his arm.

"We're from the Church of Jesus Christ of Latter Day Saints," they informed me.

"Hallelujah!" I responded. "You found me." I quickly invited the two Mormon missionaries to come inside and tell me about their church.

There are many scriptures that warn against false prophets in the Bible, those who would try to draw believers away from the truth. *"Beloved, believe not every spirit, but test the spirits whether they are of God because many false prophets have gone out into the world"* (I John 4:1). But at the time I was so lonely, I would have welcomed anyone. I was completely deceived and didn't even sense that the wolves were circling the sheepfold.

There is danger in being a little lamb away from the flock and I was caught unaware as the Mormons began to entice me with their false doctrine. I listened intently to everything the men told me about the church they represented. Remember that I was seeking a church where I could find the people of God. Perhaps this was that church.

I described my experience to the two Mormon missionaries, telling them how Jesus had saved me from my sins.

"That's wonderful," they said when I had finished my testimony. "You definitely belong in our church. We will baptize you in water and then lay hands on you so you will be filled with the Holy Spirit."

"I have already been filled with the Holy Spirit," I told them. "The Holy Spirit came upon me last March."

They seemed very surprised. "Who laid hands on you?" they asked.

"It was the Lord Jesus. He baptized me in the Holy Spirit last March while I was in my bedroom. Jesus has filled me to overflowing."

After hearing my testimony, the men weren't as eager to continue with the conversation. After taking my name and address, they left and I was once again alone wondering where my people might be found.

Little did I know that after the Mormons left my house, they went two blocks down the street and started knocking on doors again. Six houses later a pretty dark-haired woman answered their knock and talked with them briefly. Apparently she proceeded to inform them that Jesus had saved her and had also baptized her in the Holy Spirit.

They must have been really surprised and overwhelmed by the testimony she gave, because they blurted out, "You're the second woman to tell us that about that experience today. It's almost exactly the same story."

"Who is the other woman?" she asked

Without even thinking, they pulled out the card I had just filled out and gave her my name and address.

Within minutes my phone was ringing and I heard a feminine voice shouting, "Hallelujah! I've found you. Can I come over?"

Darlene turned out to be a Catholic charismatic, filled to overflowing with the Holy Spirit and the joy of the Lord. She was so bold in talking to people about Jesus that she even frightened me.

I could hardly believe it when she told me that there were thousands of people just like me all over the world. "We're what they call Charismatic Christians," she told me. "Some people even refer to us as Jesus people, and I guess that's really what we are. We're people from many different churches and denominations who love Jesus and love one another."

Giving me a big hug, Darlene added, "God is doing a new thing. He is pouring out His Spirit upon all flesh, bringing us together and making us one. We're just one big happy family no matter where we go to church."

Before Darlene left, after three beautiful hours of fellowship, she invited me to attend a Full Gospel Business Men's meeting two nights later. I didn't know how Jack would feel about me attending a men's meeting, but I really wanted to go and see what was happening there.

It was obvious that the Lord had His hand upon me, protecting me from error and guiding me into His body. Again, I could only say, "Thank You, Lord Jesus."

That night I again heard the Lord speaking to me within my heart. *"You have learned some very important lessons today, little one. My people can be found in all of the churches. You do not need to look for a church because you are The Church. My Church consists of all My people everywhere who believe in Me and have received Jesus as their Savior."*

And then God added this warning. *"Also remember that all people that use My name are not My people. Be sure that you never forget to test the spirits, My child."*

I drifted off into sleep singing the praises of God knowing that I was a part of the body of Christ.

CHAPTER 6
USE ME

Each day was a wonderful adventure as I walked hand in hand with Jesus. The beauty of creation spoke to me of the mysteries of God. Everything that I saw illustrated various principles of God's kingdom.

Late in August I spotted one little flower in full bloom on an azalea bush. I would have never expected to see a bloom so late in the season, but this little red bloom was certainly as beautiful as any of the other blossoms that had appeared in early May. In this small flower, the Lord showed me a picture of myself. I was a late spiritual bloomer, yet a thing of beauty in His eyes. It's never too late in life to open yourself to Jesus.

The snowflakes falling from the sky and covering the ground spoke to me of how Jesus had taken away my sins and made me white as snow. A rainy day depicted showers of blessing, and also reminded me of the latter rain of the Holy Spirit being poured out upon the earth. Watching the autumn leaves gently drifting down from the trees symbolized my many sins blown away by the gentle wind of the Spirit.

The world was a wonderful place. Everywhere I looked I found living parables revealing God's truths to my spirit. Fall turned into winter and winter into spring. God was renewing my mind and the old Jean was just a distant memory. Hate, anger, envy, greed were things of the past. The fruit of the Spirit was now growing in me. Joy, peace and love were evident in every aspect of my new life in Christ. Worry and anxiety were cast aside as I responded to the word of the Lord which declared, *"Don't be anxious about tomorrow"* (Matthew 6:34).

My tranquilizers and pep pills had gone the way of my cigarettes and alcohol. Even the aspirin bottle gathered dust in the medicine cabinet as the Lord ministered physical, spiritual and mental health to me.

A group of women had started gathering together in the neighborhood to study the Bible and learn more about Jesus. I soon became their teacher. God was using me to share His word. I was seeing seed that I planted in human hearts actually begin to grow. My constant prayer was, "Use me." The Lord was beginning to answer my prayer. Lives were being changed, and the life that was being changed the most was definitely mine.

One evening about seven o'clock, I prayed that the Lord would lead me to someone who really needed the love of Jesus. It didn't take long for my prayer to be answered. The very next morning, I received a call from the church asking if I was available to drive a woman into Washington for a doctor's appointment. Of course I was available. With great joy, I opened my heart and embraced this wonderful opportunity to serve.

I received Rita into my life as a gift from God. As I ministered to her over the next two years, I saw a miracle take place in her life. A woman filled with hate and bitterness, became a woman filled with love and forgiveness. A woman who was weak and infirm, became a woman glowing with health. Rita truly became a new creature in Christ Jesus.

Sometimes I look back on my ministry to Rita as on-the-job training. It wasn't always easy to deal with her anger and resentment or with her constant demands for my time and attention. It was like raising an unruly child who thought only of herself and never of others. But how many lessons I learned as I reached out to her in love. Rita will always have a special place in my heart as my first spiritual child.

I had been saved just over a year when another opportunity for ministry came along. I was approached by a woman who asked me if I would share at the World Day of Prayer being held at the local Lutheran church. Over two hundred women representing the various churches in town would be attending this gathering and it was a great honor to be invited to be the speaker. I was amazed that as a new believer, I had been chosen.

I never doubted for a moment that God was the one who had arranged for me to bring the message, but I was suddenly overcome with fear. It was one thing to teach a few women in the living room of my home and quite another to stand in the pulpit of a church and preach to two hundred people.

The last time I had been on a stage was to receive my high school diploma, and I must admit that my legs were visibly shaking as I walked across the platform. I found myself recalling a piano recital as a child when I had forgotten how to play the simple song and left the stage in disgrace. What a humiliating experience that had been. Old memories of past failures began to play across the screen of my mind. Even thinking about sharing at the service caused the butterflies in my stomach to start acting up.

I stalled for time and told the woman that I needed more time to pray about my decision, and I certainly prayed. I prayed and prayed and then prayed some more. I told God that I just couldn't do it, but when I was called for my confirmation a week later, I found myself saying yes. How could I possibly say no to God? I loved Him and wanted to please Him.

Then started the battle with Satan as the demons of fear grabbed hold of me. The Lord gave me the words for a beautiful message guaranteed to touch the hearts of the listeners, but even thinking of the upcoming day caused waves of nausea to come over me. I was nearly paralyzed with fear.

I spent hours on my knees in prayer, seeking strength to go through with this presentation. I memorized verse after verse on combating fear which I repeated to myself hundreds of times every day.

One of them was, *"Perfect love casts out all fear"* (I John 4:8). Another scripture was, *"God has not given you a spirit of fear, but of power, love and a sound mind"* (II Timothy 1:7).

I read in First Corinthians where the Apostle Paul had written, *"I was with you in weakness and in fear and in much trembling, and my speech and my preaching were not with enticing words of man's wisdom, but in demonstration of the Spirit and of power"* (I Corinthians 2:3-4).

I consoled myself with the knowledge that if the great Paul could feel such fear and overcome it through the power of God, so could I.

Three days before the church service, I started fasting. It wasn't as though I really wanted to fast or even felt the leading of the Lord to fast. It was just that I was so nervous and felt such nausea that I couldn't possibly keep a bite of food down. Talk about constant prayer! All I could manage to say to the Lord was, "Oh God, please help me!"

The morning of World Day of Prayer, I picked up the Living Bible translation of the scriptures and the pages fell open to Exodus 4:10. There I read these words written in modern-day English:

"Moses pleaded with the Lord. 'Oh Lord, I'm just not a good speaker. I never have been and I'm not one now, not even after You have spoken to me. My speech is slow and halting.'

'Who makes mouths?' Jehovah asked him. 'Isn't it I, the Lord? Who makes a man so that he can speak or not speak, see or not see, hear or not hear? Now go ahead and do as I tell you, for I will help you to speak well and I will tell you what to say.'

But Moses said, 'Lord, please! Send someone else.'

Then the Lord became angry."

Imagine that! The Lord became angry with Moses because he didn't want to become a speaker. Moses was afraid that he couldn't speak well enough to represent God and actually begged God to find someone else to take his place. Moses had faced the same fears that I was experiencing.

Something happened deep down in my heart when I read those scriptures about Moses. I certainly didn't want the Lord to be angry with me because I felt inadequate to carry out His instructions. God was with me and He wouldn't have asked me to do anything that I couldn't do. God was my strength and He was going to give me victory over the fear and insecurity that I was feeling. My faith in God was stronger than my fear.

I have to be honest and admit that, as I stepped into the pulpit, my heart was beating so wildly that I thought it would jump right out of my blouse. My mouth felt like it was filled with cotton and my skin felt cold and clammy. The spirit of fear was trying to overwhelm me.

But then I looked down upon the sea of faces waiting expectantly to hear the Word of God. Hallelujah! I knew that I had the Word to deliver to them. I opened my mouth to speak, and at that moment it was as though I was bathed in a warm light shining down from heaven. All fear was gone. Under the precious anointing of God, I brought forth the message that the Lord had given to me to deliver.

Following the service, a woman came up to me and said, "I don't know what you have inside of you, but whatever it is, I want to have it too." She began to attend my Bible study and two months later she received the Holy Spirit as I laid my hands upon her. Phyllis became one of my early disciples and was used through the years to bring many to the Lord.

Following the service that day, it was like I was floating on air. When I arrived home, I went out into the kitchen to get a drink of water. Suddenly out of the corner of my eye, I saw something fly directly toward the window and then swerve quickly upward. What was it? I ran over to look out into the back yard to see what had happened. I could hardly believe my eyes. Sitting on the edge of the bird feeder was a beautiful pure white dove, pecking away at some seed.

"Thank You, Lord," I exclaimed.

If God had opened heaven and sent down a host of angels to sing a chorus for me, it couldn't have thrilled me more. I had asked for no sign of approval from the Lord, yet He had sent the symbol of the Holy Spirit right into my own back yard.

The white dove remained in our yard for about three hours that afternoon, long enough for Jack and our children to see the wonderful sign that the Lord had sent to me as a special blessing. I still have a photo of the white dove tucked away in my top dresser drawer as a reminder of the day when I preached my first sermon.

What a mighty God we serve! A God who delights to give good gifts to His children.

CHAPTER 7

LET US WITNESS TO MILLIONS

These were days of walking with Jesus, growing spiritually stronger and gaining knowledge of the Lord and His will for me. I loved to share the Word of God and soon found myself teaching not only the group in my home, but also classes in several denominational churches.

Jack was showing definite signs of moving closer to the Lord. He had rebuffed all my efforts to get him to go to charismatic meetings, but he seemed to enjoy attending the Presbyterian church with me on Sunday mornings. I even noticed that he was occasionally peeking into the Bible and glancing at some of the Christian books I was reading.

Finally, after months of resistance, Jack broke down and agreed to attend a Full Gospel Business Men's meeting with me. The speaker was a Presbyterian minister from Pennsylvania named Jim Brown, and he brought a simple salvation message. It was a wonderful meeting and I could tell that Jack's heart was really touched through the ministry of this anointed pastor.

"I really liked what this man had to say tonight," Jack informed me on the drive home. "Maybe we should make a trip up to Pennsylvania some weekend and go to the special Saturday night meeting he has in his church."

I couldn't believe my ears! Jack was actually inviting me to go to a charismatic meeting with him. It was exceeding, abundantly above all that I could ask or think. I had spent sixteen long months believing God for Jack's salvation, and now the Holy Spirit was moving so fast that it almost took my breath away.

Less than two weeks later we were in Parksburg, Pennsylvania, sitting in Jim Brown's church on a Saturday night. The little church was crowded with people from all walks of life. There were young people, old people, hippies, men in business suits and Catholic nuns in their long black habits. Every race and nationality seemed to be represented.

As the service started, Pastor Brown came marching down the aisle playing a gigantic pair of cymbals. Everyone stood to their feet and began to praise the Lord. I looked beside me and noticed that Jack was also standing and clapping his hands in time with the music. The miracle had begun.

Not five minutes later, tears began to run down Jack's cheeks as the reality of God's love enveloped him. Jack had received Jesus as his Lord and Savior without a prayer being said, a hymn sung or even a sermon preached. My husband had been born again as He simply opened His heart in faith and received Jesus. God had answered my prayer.

As the service ended, nearly two hours later, everyone joined hands and sang the Lord's Prayer, all of their voices blending together and filling the church with the sound of a heavenly choir. In that holy moment, the wind of the spirit blew across Jack and he was baptized in the Holy Spirit. He fell into my arms weeping as Jesus filled him with power from on high.

"It's real!" Jack declared. "It's all real! Jesus has saved me and filled me with His Spirit. Jesus is alive and He has saved me."

I had a brand new husband and instantly our marriage was completely restored. We were united in one spirit, and were walking together again on the same path. Old things had passed away and all things had become new. Jesus was not only Lord of our lives, but also Lord of our marriage.

When we got back to the motel, we joined hands and prayed our first prayer together. It was a very simple prayer: "Here we are, Lord. Use us!" As we spoke those words, I knew within that God had a special plan for us waiting to be unveiled. In my heart was the sure knowledge that the Lord was going to use us as one voice in ministry. We would serve Him side by side. It was going to be Jack and Jean serving Jesus together.

The two of us were knit tightly into a new love that we had never experienced before in our marriage. Paul wrote in his letter to the Ephesian church that marriage is a great mystery (Ephesians 5:32). A Christian marriage is supposed to show a living picture to the world of the spiritual relationship between Christ and His bride, the church. Together we yielded our lives and our marriage to God and saw our house come into order.

One of the major decisions we faced was whether to remain members of the Presbyterian church that we were attending. The minister was a very compassionate man, but certainly not a spiritual man. He believed that the way into heaven was through good works, rather than through the unmerited grace of God.

"Everyone is eventually going to heaven," he informed me one day. "The Bible says that God doesn't want anyone to perish. He certainly isn't going to let anyone burn in hell for eternity. Remember, God is love."

Have you ever tried preaching the gospel to someone with a closed mind? He would patiently listen to my testimony and allow me to quote Bible verses to him, but it was like he was indulging a child. He didn't believe that the Bible was true, but merely a collection of writings from ancient times. The seeds of truth I was attempting to plant in his heart, just couldn't take root in his hardened heart. It was difficult not to get discouraged.

Was it time for us to find another church? We just didn't know what the Lord wanted us to do. And when you don't know what to do, the thing to always do is to go to God in prayer. The Bible says, *"If any man lacks wisdom, let him ask of God who gives to all men liberally"* (James 1:5).

"Lord, do You want us to leave this church or do You want us to stay where we are?" we asked in faith. "We want to do Your will, but we just don't know what Your will is. Please give us a sign. We need to have some divine direction."

It was only a few days later when the minister called to inform me that he had found someone else to take the Sunday morning class I was teaching.

"We just don't see eye to eye on a lot of things," he stated. "I really think the two of you would be happier in another church."

Talk about a sign! It was pretty obvious that the Lord had removed us from the Presbyterian church. We didn't know where He wanted us to go, but we did have confidence that He would lead and guide us.

Sometimes God says stay and sometimes God says go. Sometimes God says now and sometimes God says later. As believers we can have confidence that *"the steps of a good man are ordered by the Lord"* (Psalm 37:23). Here's some good advice: Always follow the Shepherd.

As we waited for further instructions from the Lord, we visited many different churches in the area and discovered just how big the body of Christ really is. Jesus Christ is Lord of THE Church. We felt at home everywhere that the gospel was preached, and recognized that the Lord was enlarging our vision. When you love God, you will also love His people, and you will find that His people are everywhere. We sensed that our calling was going to be to the larger body of Christ, not just to one church or one locality.

I had a habit of walking around the house praying out loud, "Lord, let me witness to millions all around the world."

Jack would often rebuke me. "That certainly isn't a very humble prayer, Jean. You shouldn't pray like that."

"But, Honey," I would respond, "the Lord told us to carry the gospel to all nations and that means millions of people. So that's what I want to do. I want to witness to millions."

God hears our prayers and He answers. If you pray little prayers, you will get little answers. If you pray big prayers, you will get big answers. I'm the kind of person that likes big answers. The Lord says in His word, *"You have not because you ask not"* (James 4:2). So I am always asking Him for all sorts of things. After all, my Father has a storehouse in heaven and He is just waiting to share His blessings with me. Just like I delight to give gifts to my children, God also delights to give good gifts to His children.

I have always admired the way the prophet Elijah prayed big prayers in the Old Testament. One time he prayed that it wouldn't rain for three and a half years, and the Lord heard and answered. For three and a half years not one drop of rain fell upon the parched ground. That's what I call a big answer to a big prayer.

So I continued to pray day after day, "Lord, let us witness to millions." You notice that I was no longer praying, "Let me witness.' My prayer had been changed to, "Let us witness." Now that Jack was growing in the spirit, I knew that the Lord was ready to use him in ministry also.

In August of 1973, Jack and I were invited to appear on *"God's Good News,"* a local television program sponsored by the Full Gospel Business Men. The program was beamed into seven million homes in the Washington area every week. Jack was only one hundred days old in the Lord when we faced the television cameras and shared with the viewers how the Lord had changed our lives. As we stepped out in faith, the doors were opening.

We started holding weekly charismatic meetings in our home on Thursday evenings. Before we really knew what had happened, not only were all the chairs filled, but also most of the floor. People sat up the stairs, on the kitchen counters and even under the dining room table. Young and old alike showed up at our front door drawn by the Holy Spirit. Soon between eighty and ninety people were showing up at our small home every week to praise the Lord together. In the next five years, over a thousand people were saved and filled with the Holy Spirit at the Thursday praise gathering.

I recall one evening when there was a knock at the front door during the meeting. A young man was standing there and asked if our daughter was at home. I didn't even answer his question, but simply said, "Come on in. We're having a prayer meeting and the Lord wants you to join us."

He hesitated for a few moments, then came in and sat on the floor near the front door. The power of the Holy Spirit was so strong that night that you could physically feel the presence of the Lord. The Shekinah glory filled the house, and with hands lifted to heaven, we all praised God.

After about an hour, the boy stood up and announced, "I want to know this Jesus too. Will someone pray with me?" And another lamb was added to the Lord's flock. What can one do but worship and adore!

One of the greatest miracles was to see the Lord raise up my husband as a man of God and an elder in the body of Christ. Overnight he was transformed into a person of holiness, living completely for the Lord Jesus Christ. Words of love, wisdom and knowledge flowed forth from him as God smoothed away the rough edges and polished him, preparing Jack for service in the kingdom of God.

I found myself married to a completely new man. *"Old things had passed away and all things had become new"* (II Corinthians 5:17). Jack was a man with a shepherd's heart and with the love of God flowing freely through him. His outer appearance even changed and people started asking him if he was a minister. It was obvious that Jack was a Christian. Many people don't realize that the word "Christian" means Christ-like. When you say you are a Christian, you are actually saying that you are like Christ. A prayer that Jack and I often prayed together was, "Let others be able to see Christ in us. Make us like Jesus."

Together we walked God's chosen path, not knowing where it was leading, but eager to be about our Father's business. We found ourselves being invited to speak in churches and meetings all around the area. As we preached the gospel, we saw people saved. As we laid lands upon the sick, we saw people healed. Signs and wonders were following us because we believed, and when you believe, with God all things are possible.

CHAPTER 8

IN EVERYTHING GIVE THANKS

Then in October 1973, disaster struck. One Saturday morning Jack called me into the living room and calmly said, "Pray for me. I'm having another heart attack."

Quickly I laid my hands upon him and said, "You blood clot, I curse you in the name of Jesus and demand that you dissolve. And now Lord, I come to You in Jesus' name, and ask that Your healing power flow into Jack. Heal his heart, Father."

A little over an hour later, we were at Holy Cross Hospital and Jack was once again in coronary care wired up to everything imaginable. There was a sense of unreality as we both tried to grasp what had happened. My brand new Christian husband was having a heart attack. How could this be? We were just starting to do the Lord's work together and now he was lying helpless in a hospital bed.

The doctors assured me that there was no immediate danger, so I headed back home to spend a little time with the children. Just the day before I had finished reading a book called, "Power in Praise." The book stressed a verse of scripture which states, *"In everything give thanks for this is the will of God in Christ*

Jesus concerning you" (Thessalonians 5:18). So as I drove along the Beltway, I started talking with the Lord.

"Thank You, Father. I don't pretend to understand why Jack has had this heart attack, but I know that You are the One who heals the broken hearted. I do believe that *"all things work together for good for those who love God and are called according to His purpose"* (Romans 8:28). Lord, I do love You and I know that You have called Jack and me to serve You. So right now I place Jack into Your capable hands and give You praise."

As I continued my journey home, I began to sing songs of praise. I must admit that tears were working their way down my cheeks as I lifted my voice to the Lord. But fifteen minutes later, as I pulled into the driveway, I was singing a chorus directly from the Bible, *"Rejoice in the Lord always, and again I say rejoice"* (Philippians 4:4).

Fear, depression, apprehension and doubt had vanished. As I sang praises, God had given me the gift of faith. I knew Jack was going to get well. I knew something wonderful was going to come out of this heart problem. I knew that God was in control of the entire situation. Inwardly and outwardly I was rejoicing and was filled to overflowing with joy and a knowledge of the goodness of God. I was truly experiencing the peace that passes all understanding that is described in the Bible. That night I slept like a baby, knowing that the Father was watching over Jack.

Visiting hours are very limited in a coronary care unit and I was only allowed to spend ten minutes with Jack every hour. The other fifty minutes were spent in the intensive care waiting room where I shared about Jesus with those who were also waiting to see their loved ones. The Lord had provided me with a captive audience.

Every day I would arrive at the hospital with a big smile and the joy of the Lord. The people there would look at me in amazement and ask, "How can you be so happy with your young husband in coronary care?" That question would be just the opening I needed to tell them about Jesus.

Lunch time was spent at cafeteria tables sharing about Jesus with my many new friends. Time passed slowly in the small waiting room, so I loaded my purse with gospel tracts so everyone would have something to read. I was able to pray with several of the women to receive Jesus.

One afternoon at the hospital, I heard the Lord speak to me and say, *"Jean, I want you to go down to the chapel and pray."*

"But, Lord," I replied. "I don't need to go downstairs to the chapel to pray. You are here with me and I can pray just as well right where I am."

"I said I wanted you to go down to the chapel to pray."

"Yes, Lord."

As I entered the door of the chapel, I heard the sounds of someone crying. There, kneeling at the altar rail, was an older woman, and I knew immediately why I was there. The Lord had just finished telling me that He wanted me to pray in the chapel, and I knew I had been sent to pray with her.

Quickly I walked down the aisle and knelt next to her. "The Lord sent me here to pray with you," I said as I slipped my arm around her shoulder.

"I can hardly believe this," she replied. "I just told the Lord that I needed someone to agree with me in prayer and here you are. My mother is very ill and I'm so worried about her. Please pray with me that God will heal her."

Two believers brought together in a hospital chapel. A small miracle perhaps, but just an example of how God leads and guides us. Amazing things can happen when we listen and obey. Whatever He says to you, do it.

There was good news about Jack. He was doing so well that the doctors were amazed. Of course, Jack lost no opportunity to tell them the reason for his recovery was because of the Great Physician.

It certainly looked like we had the victory. Jack was transferred out of coronary care and into a private room. What a time of rejoicing. The doctors were calling it a false alarm and telling us that Jack could go home in just a day or two.

Then suddenly everything changed. An irregular heartbeat had shown up on the EKG and the doctors were very concerned about the abnormality. At first it was just an extra heartbeat every few minutes, but then the beats kept increasing and increasing. I arrived at the hospital to find Jack waiting to be moved back into the coronary care unit.

"Honey," he asked me, "what's gone wrong? We were so sure that the Lord had healed me. What happened?"

I had no answer either. I felt like I had just been hit in the stomach with a closed fist. Just the previous night, I had testified at a large meeting about Jack's miraculous healing. Satan was trying to make a liar out of me, and out of God.

It was a bad scene. Jack's color was ashen and he was so heavily sedated that he was hardly making any sense. The future didn't exactly look rosy and God seemed to be a million miles away. I knew that He was still with us, but the conscious knowledge of His presence seemed to have been withdrawn.

"Lord, send me a ministering angel," I pleaded. "You sent me to pray with the woman in the chapel. Now please send someone to pray with me."

Turning my back on Jack so he wouldn't see my tears, I walked across his room to the open door. Directly across from Jack's room were the elevators, and one of the elevator doors was just opening. To my surprise, a man Jack and I had recently met at a prayer meeting stepped off the elevator.

"Well, hello there," he remarked as he recognized me. "It's good to see you again. How are you?"

My ministering angel had arrived in the form of a Spirit-filled believer named Stan Nichols.

"Please come pray for Jack," I implored him. "He's had a heart attack and it looks like his heart is going into fibrillation. They're getting ready to transfer him back to coronary care."

Without hesitation, Stan followed me into Jack's room. He raised one hand to heaven and bellowed out, "Father, in the name and the power of the Lord Jesus Christ, I take control of this entire situation. I come against this spirit of infirmity and command it to leave right now. Death, get your hands off of this servant of God. Jack belongs to God and you will not have him."

Then, placing both of his hands upon Jack's chest, he said, "I release the healing power of God into this body. Be healed in Jesus' name."

Waves of the Holy Spirit flowed over me as the power of God filled the room. We were surrounded by His mighty presence. Faith in the healing grace of the Lord Jesus was almost overwhelming. All doubt was dispelled. Right there in the hospital room, the three of us had experienced a visitation from Almighty God. I knew that the Lord had touched Jack and that he was healed. Jack would live to serve the Lord.

My ministering angel didn't have wings or a halo, but I know that Stan was sent by God in answer to my prayer.

"God bless you both," Stan said as he turned to leave. "I'm glad you were at the door when I got off of the elevator."

With a smile, I replied, "I'm glad you were on the elevator."

What an awesome God we serve!

CHAPTER 9

AND THY HOUSE

Jack was moved back into coronary care, and I went home. It was Thursday evening when the prayer and praise meeting was always held at our house. These meetings continue on regardless of circumstances. Whenever Jack and I are out of town, we leave the key with someone because God will bring the people whether we are home or not. The meetings also go on whether we are sick or not. When you give your house to God for His use, you can be sure that He will use it.

Jack and I have three children, two girls and a boy. At the time of Jack's heart attack, John was thirteen, Debbie was sixteen, and Kathy, who was away at college, was eighteen.

Three months before Jack became ill, our son had received Jesus as his Savior at the local Baptist church. We were very surprised that morning when John announced that he wasn't going to go with us to the Presbyterian church, but wanted to attend the Baptist church instead.

"That's no problem," Jack told him. "We'll just all go together to the Baptist church."

John shook his head. "No, I don't want you to go with me. I want to go there alone. It's not very far and I'll just ride my bicycle over there."

Sometimes you just give up trying to figure out thirteen-year-olds, so we just gave our approval and went our separate ways.

When we arrived home from church several hours later, John was sitting on the couch in the living room waiting for us. "I accepted Jesus as my Lord and Savior today," he informed us. "When the minister gave the altar call, I went up front and gave my heart to Jesus. I wanted to ask Jesus in before, but the Presbyterian church never had an altar call so I didn't know what to do."

John seemed to breathe a sigh of relief. "But He's in there now. When I saw how happy the two of you were after Jesus came into your hearts, I wanted Him to live in me too. So I invited Him in this morning and He came in. I got saved."

What do you say at a time like that? We just put our arms around our newborn son and rejoiced in the Lord together.

I must admit that I did ask myself why I hadn't personally given John the opportunity to pray the sinner's prayer with me. Sometimes we close our eyes to the needs of our own family because we are so busy reaching out to the needs of others. It's comforting to know that although we may let others down, God is always there to pick them up.

But then, maybe this was something that John needed to do on his own. Perhaps he had to take his own personal step of faith toward Jesus without holding onto my hand. I guess I'll never really know.

Our girls had still not received Jesus at the time of Jack's heart problem, but we had claimed them both for His kingdom. There was that Bible verse again, *"Believe on the Lord Jesus Christ and you will be saved and your house"* (Acts 16:31).

On the Thursday night when the prayer meeting was held, Jack was still in the hospital. John had decided to attend the meeting, but Debbie was locked upstairs in her bedroom, rebelling against the influx of "religious fanatics" that she felt had taken over the house.

There were about fifteen young "Jesus people" from the other side of town who had come to the meeting for the very first time. What a wonderful gathering of God's people was taking place. Perhaps there were thirty or forty believers who had come together to worship the Lord.

The Holy Spirit was in charge that night to a degree never before seen in our home. The young people had brought their guitars and the praise was glorious. We all started lifting our voices to God, singing the psalms directly from the Bible and experiencing God in our midst.

Suddenly one of the young men said, "Sister, we should pray for your husband's healing in proxy tonight." I wasn't even sure what proxy meant.

The next thing I knew, I was sitting on a chair in the middle of the living room with dozens of hands laid upon me. As prayers were being offered up for Jack, heaven came and glory filled our souls. The Lord poured out His love upon everyone who was assembled. It was an awesome demonstration of the power of God.

Then suddenly we heard sobs coming from the corner of the room, growing in intensity. It was my son, John, and I quickly rose from the chair and went over to him.

"It's all right," I said, seeking to comfort John. "Your dad is going to get well. He's not going to die. Everything is going to be all right. He'll be home with us soon."

John continued to sob. "I know that. That's not why I'm crying. Jesus just baptized me in the Holy Spirit. It was just like a giant bubble burst inside of me and it's so wonderful. Jesus baptized me tonight, Mom!"

Thank You, Jesus. As John continued sharing his testimony, voices were raised and everyone began to sing in the spirit, their voices blending together in perfect harmony. It was a sound that reached up to heaven, a new song sung by those who have been redeemed through the blood of Jesus, the Lamb of God.

The next morning I was able to bring good news to Jack at the hospital. He now had a Spirit-filled son.

The following Sunday morning, Debbie, our daughter, surprised me by agreeing to go to church with John and me. By this time, we had found an Assembly of God church that we were attending fairly regularly. For over a year, Debbie had flatly refused to go to church or even discuss Jesus with us, but that morning, when I asked her to go, she agreed almost enthusiastically.

When we got to the church, we found out that it was the first day of revival meetings and there was a guest evangelist who would be preaching. He approached the pulpit, looked out over the congregation and declared, "The Lord has just told me that there are several unsaved people here this morning, so I'm not going to preach. Instead, we're all going to pray until God saves them."

Everyone began to pray. Ten minutes later, Debbie got out of the pew and walked down the aisle to the altar rail. There, with tears streaming down her face, she knelt and gave her heart to Jesus. The Lord gave our Debbie the gift of eternal life, and the love of God shone from her as we left the church.

The three of us got into the car and drove directly to the hospital with more good news for Jack. This time I was able to tell him that he had a saved daughter. Would the wonders of God never cease? Of course not!

Three nights later, Debbie, John and I decided to attend another one of the revival meetings that were still going on at the church. That Wednesday evening the evangelist preached on the baptism of the Holy Spirit and how it is God's will that everyone receive power to witness for Him.

The next thing I knew, Debbie was once again on her way to the altar, and five minutes later she was filled to overflowing with the Holy Spirit, praising God in the new language that He had given her.

More good news for Jack! In the two weeks while he recuperated in the hospital, his son had been saved, and both his son and daughter had been baptized in the Spirit. *"All things work together for good to them that love God . . ."* (Romans 8:28).

Later Debbie told us that on the night of the prayer meeting, she had unlocked her bedroom door and crept out into the upstairs hall. Unobserved, she had listened to everything that was going on downstairs. When she heard everyone singing in the spirit, her heart had been strangely touched. Debbie had started to cry and throughout the night, she kept waking up. In her mind she would keep hearing the heavenly singing and then would cry some more. "I suddenly knew that it was all real," Debbie said. "I knew that Jesus loved me and wanted to forgive my sins."

How amazing is God's love. *"God so loved the world that He gave His only begotten Son, that whosoever would believe in Him, would not perish but have everlasting life"* (John 3:16). Such a familiar verse, but when you actually believe that verse, it will open the door into heaven.

On Friday morning, Jack received more good news, this time from the doctor. The extra heartbeat had completely disappeared and there was no new heart damage. Even more miraculous, the damage from the previous heart attack appeared to have disappeared. His heart was beating strongly in perfect rhythm, so there was no reason to keep him in the hospital any longer

"Jesus has healed me," Jack informed his two Jewish doctors. "I told you that your Messiah was going to heal my heart, and now He has done it."

Jack was released from the hospital at seven-thirty in the morning and at seven-thirty that same evening, he was speaking at a meeting in a Methodist church with the good news that Jesus was not only his Savior and Baptizer, but also his Healer.

CHAPTER 10

BROKEN LOAVES

When Jack got out of the hospital it seemed as though God had moved us onto an entirely new plateau. Jack was not only strong physically, but also spiritually. People from all denominations seemed to gravitate to him for ministry. Day by day I could see him grow in wisdom and boldness.

One day I happened to turn on the television set to a new program that was being shown in Washington called "The 700 Club." I sat on the arm of a chair for about ten minutes watching it and then I prayed, "Lord, please allow the two of us go on that program to witness for You."

Three weeks later the phone rang with a long distance call from Portsmouth, Virginia. It was an invitation for us to appear as guests on "The 700 Club." Thank You, Jesus. God wasn't going to forget my prayer that we be allowed to witness to millions.

We were going to drive to Portsmouth, which was about four and a half hours away from where we lived, and spend the night there. The program was to be broadcast live at eight o'clock in the evening, and it was suggested that we be at the station about an hour prior to the broadcast to have time to get acquainted with the host of the program.

It was a beautiful day in January when we headed off for our television adventure. Plenty of time had been allowed for the drive and an early dinner before we needed to arrive at the studio. We sang all the way down to Virginia, rejoicing in the wonderful things that God had done for us and praising him for the opportunity to appear on the program.

About forty miles from Portsmouth, we noticed smoke coming out from beneath the hood of the car. By the time we had found a gas station, we looked like a little white cloud rolling down the road.

The Lord had led us to a small station operated by two elderly Christian men who loved Jesus. Fanning away the smoke, they opened the hood and looked inside. We waited anxiously for their verdict.

"It looks really bad," they informed us. "Apparently you've hit a stone that has caused a big hole in your radiator, but we'll see what we can do to get you back on your way."

I knew what I could do. I could pray. There was no doubt in my mind that the Lord wanted us to appear on the program. Everything was going to be fine. This was just an attack of the devil and a testing of our faith. God was certainly on our side. I recalled a Bible verse that said, *"The battle is not yours, but God's"* (II Chronicles 20:15).

Patiently we waited as can after can of Stop-Leak was poured into the radiator and leaked right back out. I was trying to give thanks in all things, but the situation seemed to be getting worse instead of better.

Finally the mechanic shook his head in defeat. "I'm sorry, but it's hopeless. The only way to get this car back on the road is to replace the radiator. I have one available, but it will take several hours to make the necessary repair."

At that time it was after six-thirty and we were still forty miles away from our destination. I was starting to lose hope, but Jack was standing firm believing that the Lord was still going to supply our need. Then suddenly, we realized, our need had already been met.

Jack's eyes were drawn to a car that was parked over by the side of the garage. It was an old beat-up car that was probably close to thirty years old. The chrome bumpers were showing some rust and the body was badly in need of a paint job, but it looked like it could run.

Without a second thought, Jack asked, "Does that car run? Would you be willing to rent it to us so we can get to Portsmouth? We'll pay you and get it back to you tomorrow morning. Can you help us?"

"Well, she may not look like much but she's a good old car," the mechanic answered, "She'll get you there safely, so don't you worry about it. You don't need to pay me anything. Let's just call it a gift. Now go ahead and put your suitcases in the car while I fill her up with gas."

Just a few minutes later we were in the car and on our way down the road to Portsmouth. I guess we were feeling a little like Jesus must have felt when He rode into Jerusalem on a borrowed donkey.

God's timing is always perfect. The theme song of the program was just starting to play as we walked into the studio. We were right on time to tell the millions how much we loved Jesus and how He had filled our lives with love, joy and peace. God can make a way when there seems to be no way. God can solve a problem when there seems to be no solution. Never underestimate the power of God.

Oh, the joy of sharing Jesus. It's the modern-day method of feeding the multitude. Have you ever really pondered what the Bible has recorded about the time Jesus fed over five thousand people? It must be a very important miracle because it's the only one that's included in each of the four gospels. That makes it very special in my eyes.

"Jesus commanded the multitude to sit down on the grass. Then He took the five loaves and the two fish, and looking up to heaven, He blessed the loaves and then broke them and gave them to His disciples. And His disciples gave them to the multitude. When everyone had eaten and was full, the disciples gathered up the fragments that remained and there were twelve baskets full" (Matthew 14:19-20).

Look at that and consider carefully what happened. Jesus broke the loaves and gave them to His disciples to pass out to the people. Jesus supplied the bread, but it was the disciples who actually gave it to the crowd.

Hallelujah! Jesus, the Bread of Life, has allowed His body to be broken for us, and now we have the Bread of Life. We have been given Jesus and our responsibility is to share Him with others. He has called us to feed the multitude. Jesus is the broken Bread that we are responsible to distribute to the masses. We are to witness so that all men everywhere might also feed upon the spiritual bread that provides spiritual life.

Did you realize that there were twelve baskets of bread left over? Twelve disciples and twelve baskets of bread. No disciple left empty-handed. A disciple will always have a fresh supply of spiritual bread available to be shared with any spiritually hungry person that might be encountered.

It's such a blessing to be able to tell people about Jesus. I consider the grocery store to be my mission field. It's always exciting to go shopping because I know that the Lord is going to have someone there who needs to hear about Jesus. Before I walk through the door of the supermarket, my prayer always is, "Lord, give me an opportunity to witness today. Lead me to a ready heart where I can plant a spiritual seed."

And He always does. Some remarkable things have happened in the aisles of my local grocery store. One day I had nearly finished my shopping without meeting anyone with whom to share the love of the Lord.

"Isn't there anyone in the store who is hungry for spiritual things?" I asked the Lord. "You're going to have to show me who you have put in my path today because I'm just nearly ready to go to the checkout counter."

Within two seconds, as I rounded the corner of the aisle, I was face to face with a woman I recognized from my neighborhood. I couldn't even remember her name, but I knew the Lord had brought us together.

"How are you today?" I inquired, opening the conversation.

"Not really very well," was her reply. "My thirteen-year-old daughter is being admitted to Children's Hospital in Boston tomorrow for brain surgery. They have discovered a tumor in Nancy's brain that is causing her to have seizures. The surgeon has told us that removing the growth may leave her partially paralyzed, but this is just a chance we have to take. There is nothing else that we can do."

I reached out and took hold of her hand. "There's certainly one thing that we can do. We can pray and believe together that the surgery will be successful and that there will be no damage to Nancy's brain. Jesus is alive and still healing people today. He healed my husband and I know that He can heal your daughter."

I could sense a glimmer of hope rising up within her. "I believe in God," she replied, "and I know that God can heal Nancy if that's His will."

"Of course it's His will. He doesn't want to see Nancy sick anymore than you do. God answers my prayers and I'm certainly going to pray for your daughter's healing."

As I spoke those words, I heard the voice of God speaking to me from within. *"I want you pray for her right now here in the grocery store."*

There we stood, directly behind the checkout counter, surrounded by the many shoppers in a crowded grocery store.

"Let's pray right now," I said taking her hand. We closed our eyes and bowed our heads, shutting out the world around us.

I don't remember what I prayed, but I do know that as I reached out to the Lord, I was given the gift of faith. I knew that Nancy would be healed. I knew that the surgery was going to be a success and that there would be no permanent injury to her brain. When you reach out in faith and touch God, you have an assurance in your heart that your prayer will be answered.

When I finished praying, our eyes were wet with tears. We had forgotten all about the shoppers around us because we had just been in the very throne room of God. No matter where you are, it's always the right time and the right place to pray. Don't ever put it off until later.

Several days later I received a phone call from Boston informing me that Nancy had come through the surgery without any problems. The doctors were calling it a miracle. There was no paralysis and no brain damage. Nancy could expect to live a normal life with no further complications.

The love and mercy of God stagger the imagination. God will work anywhere that your faith allows Him entrance. He will minister through you at the office, in a hospital, in a church, at the beach or on an airplane. When you are a disciple, the Lord will bring people with needs into your life, but you must be alert to His leading and yield to His Spirit. Yes, even when you're pushing a shopping cart through the grocery store.

CHAPTER 11

DEAD AND BURIED

I hate sin! When a Christian is born again, he puts on the nature of Christ. As sin is repulsive to Jesus, it is also repulsive to the child of God. Many people don't understand what happens to our old nature when we receive Jesus. When I approached the cross seeking forgiveness for my sins, I saw Jesus hanging on the front of the cross and an empty space on the back. I knew that the empty spot was reserved for me. My old sin nature had to be crucified. The person I used to be had to be put to death.

This is how the Apostle Paul was able to say, *"I am crucified with Christ: nevertheless I live, yet not I, but it is Christ who lives in me"* (Galatians 2:20).

Once the old man is dead, the next step is to bury that person and his evil nature. This is the purpose of water baptism. The water represents the grave, a burial place for the old sinful nature. As you are lowered into the water, it signifies the burial of your old man, and when you are raised up out of the water, it depicts your resurrection into new life in Christ Jesus. The simplicity of it is so beautiful.

From that day on you can say to your old evil nature when it starts to act up again, "Oh no you don't! I left you buried back there in the waters of baptism. You are dead and buried and have no place in me." Then you can move forward in victory.

Shortly after Jack was saved, the Lord began speaking to us about water baptism. Although I had poured water on Jack's head the night he was saved in Pennsylvania, he wasn't satisfied with only a light sprinkling. And I wasn't content with my prior baptism either. As we carefully studied the scriptures, we saw a definite pattern emerge: believe and be baptized.

At the age of sixteen, I had been baptized in a Baptist church. Several members of the youth group were being baptized and I decided that I wanted to be baptized too. I went into the water a dry sinner and came out a wet sinner. My decision to be baptized had nothing to do with believing in Jesus as my Savior. It had been a mockery and blasphemy for I had taken the Lord's name in vain.

Many are able to quote the third commandment that says, *"Thou shall not take the name of the Lord thy God in vain, for the Lord will not hold him guiltless that takes His name in vain"* (Exodus 20:7). I always thought that particular verse was referring to swear words, using the Lord's name as a curse, but that isn't the meaning at all. How many people are walking around calling themselves Christians when they are not true believers? That's what the Bible is referring to when it speaks of taking the Lord's name in vain.

On a summer's evening in August, Jack and I were water baptized along with our son in an Assembly of God church. Eleven believers went into the waters of baptism that night. There were three Presbyterians, two Methodists, two Lutherans and four members from the local Assembly of God.

Suddenly all of the "fish" were swimming together in the mighty river of God. The barriers between denominations were coming down and we were being united by the Spirit of God. Church leaders have been attempting for years to bring God's people together, but the Lord is doing it today through the ministry of the Holy Spirit.

I'll never forget that night when I buried the old man. The water felt warm and refreshing as I stepped down into it.

"Do you love the Lord?" the minister asked me.

"I love Him with all of my heart."

"And do you acknowledge Jesus as your personal Savior?

"Yes, Jesus is my Savior. I believe that He died on the cross for my sins and I'll follow Him for as long as I live."

I closed my eyes and felt myself being lowered into the water. As the water closed in over me, I was surrounded by God's love. It was like the arms of God were wrapped around me there in the watery grave. And then suddenly I was being lifted up out of the water and the joy that flooded my soul was beyond description.

"Praise the Lord!" I shouted, as I stood there in the water laughing and crying all at once. The old man was buried. The funeral service was over. As I climbed the steps out of the tank I knew that *"old things had passed away and all things had become new"* (II Corinthians 5:17).

Then to make my joy complete, I was able to watch my husband and son also go into the waters of baptism. Talk about a cup running over! What does one say? Thank You, Jesus!

The old man is dead, yet occasionally he will try to rise up and take over the throne of our hearts again. We have to crucify him daily to make sure that he stays dead and buried.

One day at the shopping center, as I was backing my car out of a tight parking space, I suddenly heard a loud scraping sound. Obviously I had been too close to the car next to me. There was nothing to do but pull forward, and when I did, there it was again. Scrunch! I got out of the car and surveyed the damage. Two long scratches were running along the door of the other car.

As I stood there in the parking lot examining the car door, I looked around and was astonished to see that my mishap had attracted no attention. The noise of the collision had sounded like a major earthquake in my ears, but no one else had even noticed. I expected people to come running over to see what had happened, but there was no one. I stood there alone in the parking lot unobserved by the passing scene.

"No one saw you, Jean. You can get in your car and drive away and no one will ever know about the accident."

Clearly I heard a voice speaking to me. "Jack will really be upset about this. You know how he is always teasing you about your driving? You'll never live this down, and don't forget that accident last year when you skidded on the ice into another car. This will make two claims in less than a year. You might even lose your insurance."

What the voice was saying made sense to me.

"Get in the car and leave," the voice continued. "No one will ever know what happened."

I looked around. No one was in sight.

"Hurry," the voice commanded. "Go now before someone comes."

Quickly I got into my car, backed out of the parking place and drove away from the shopping center.

"You've got it made now," the voice stated. "You're home free."

Then I heard another voice, this time a still small voice speaking in the depth of my heart. *"Jean, what have you done?"*

"Oh God," I called out. "What have I done?"

Even as I spoke those words, I felt the loss of communion with the Lord. There I was in willful sin, driving down the street away from the scene of the crime. I had listened to the old serpent, just like Eve did in the garden of Eden. The devil had deceived me.

"Father, forgive me," I cried out. "Lord, please keep that car in the parking lot until I have a chance to remedy this wrong I have done."

I executed a U-turn and drove back to the shopping center. For the first time since I had been born again, I had knowingly gone against the will of God and my heart was breaking.

"Lord, I'm so sorry for what I did and by Your grace, I'll never do anything like that again." It was the prayer of a repentant child.

"If we confess our sins, He is faithful and just to forgive us our sins and to cleanse us from all unrighteousness" (I John 2:1).

As I turned to God asking forgiveness, I felt the cleansing of His blood and His peace filling my heart once again. I knew I had been restored and that I was once more right with the Lord.

Now I needed to see if I could make it right with the owner of the car. I was relieved to see that the car with the scratched door was still parked in the same spot. Obviously the owner hadn't returned and discovered the damage. The Lord had answered my prayer and granted me an opportunity to make amends for my mistake.

Quickly I wrote a short note to the car's owner. "I'm sorry that I damaged your car. Please call me." I left my name and phone number, tucked the note securely under the windshield wiper and drove off thanking God for His goodness and mercy.

I was forgiven, and when God forgives us, we must also forgive ourselves. I know many believers who are still mourning over sins that they committed in the past, but when God forgives, He also forgets. We must do the same. Learn to say, "Thank You, Lord," after you confess your sins, and then go on your way rejoicing.

When I got home, I called Jack at the office and told him what had happened. Satan had definitely lied to me because

Jack wasn't angry about what had occurred in the parking lot. He knew that it was an accident and was very understanding. In fact, he was even sympathetic about my mishap.

It was about two hours later when the phone rang. "Mrs. Coleman? My name is Dan McAllister and I found your note on my car."

My voice was a little shaky as I tried to apologize. "I'm so sorry about what happened. As I was backing out, I accidently scraped the side of your car and you can see that I damaged the door."

"Yes, I noticed the scratches as I got into the car," he replied. "When I got home, I took a bucket of warm soapy water and a sponge to wipe off the door and determine the extent of the damage. This is really pretty amazing, but when I ran the sponge over the scratches, they completely washed off. There's no damage at all to the car."

I couldn't believe my ears. "Are you sure?"

"I'm positive," he insisted. "There's absolutely nothing wrong with the car. It must have just been some paint from your car that rubbed off on the door. Whatever it was, it's gone now."

"Praise the Lord!" I responded. "Are you sure you don't want me to notify my insurance company?"

"There's certainly no reason to do that. There's not any damage to report. Actually, the reason that I called was to thank you for leaving your name. Most people wouldn't have done that. They would have just driven away."

"I'm a Christian," I informed him, feeling the love of God surge through me. "I suspect we have just witnessed a miracle with your car."

He laughed. "I wouldn't be too surprised."

What a wonderful Savior! Not only did Jesus forgive me for my sin, but He removed all evidence of damage from the car, and even gave me an opportunity to witness. No wonder I love Him so much.

I went outside and took a closer look at my car to see where it might be missing some paint. It wasn't. Praise the Lord!

I learned a valuable lesson from that experience. Christians must always be on guard against Satan. We need to be alert at all times. I took my eyes off of Jesus and turned them onto a damaged car. Instead of thinking of others, I had thought only of saving myself.

When you face a problem, don't forget to ask yourself what Jesus would do if He was in the same situation. Then, go ahead and do it.

CHAPTER 12
SILVER AND GOLD

The Christian life should be filled with miracles. No day should pass without the hand of God being evident in your life. How hard it is to single out a few episodes of the Spirit-filled life to share. A life with Jesus is filled with surprises and you never know what to expect. Marriage counseling books always advise husbands to surprise their wives occasionally with candy, flowers or even a pretty nightgown. Our Heavenly Husband knows that secret and He is constantly showering blessings upon His Bride.

There is no doubt in my mind that *"God is able to supply all my needs according to His riches in glory by Christ Jesus"* (Philippians 4:19). He has demonstrated the truth of that verse over and over. All that His children have to do is ask, believing.

Our oldest daughter was registered at the local university preparing to commute to college from home. It was really all that our wallet could afford. But what Kathy really wanted to do was to go away to school. She envisioned a small college somewhere down South, but it was out of the question financially. We made too much money to qualify for aid and not enough money to afford to pay for her schooling on our own. But of course, we weren't on our own. We had the Lord.

Kathy was standing in the hall outside the guidance office one afternoon when the counselor noticed her and motioned for her to come inside.

"You're a Presbyterian, aren't you?" the counselor asked. "There's a representative here from a small southern Presbyterian college and no one has made an appointment to see him. Why don't you talk with him for a few minutes? You're a good student so perhaps he would grant you a scholarship."

Two weeks later we received a letter from the college offering Kathy an academic scholarship that was enough to cover one-third of her tuition, as well as her room and board. What a tremendous blessing. Of course, we still needed the other two-thirds, but we had faith that God was going to provide for everything. In faith we sent in Kathy's application and deposit.

God didn't seem to be concerned at all about the additional money that was still required. He simply put it in my mother's mind to sent a very large check to help with the expense of Kathy's education. In fact, her check arrived the day after we mailed in the college application. We hadn't asked my mother for money or even mentioned the need to her. God has a way of moving upon someone's heart and using them to carry out His will.

Three days later, God used the mailman to deliver God's answer to our prayer for the remaining money that was needed. Our income tax refund for the year was overwhelming. It was three times as much as we had ever received before. Why was it so much more? Because, we had started tithing to the church. You can never outgive God.

It was amazing to see how the Lord continued to work things out. As a rule, freshmen were not allowed to hold a job. However, the school informed us that Kathy was such an excellent student that they were offering her a job on campus. Result? She made enough money to cover all of her personal needs while she was at college.

Problem? Kathy would need transportation money to travel the five hundred miles back and forth from home. God's solution? She was consistently offered rides with friends. All she had to do was chip in a few dollars each trip to help pay for gas.

Our Kathy went through four years of college and God provided for everything. Following her graduation, the school even sent us a refund. I won't even attempt to describe how the Lord managed that. Let's just say it was another miracle from a miracle-working God.

Our God provides in many interesting ways. We have always been a one income family, which means that there is never much reserve in our bank account. I quickly learned that the Lord didn't want me to feel secure because I had lots of money in the bank. He wanted me to feel secure because I had Jesus in my heart. What a great revelation!

God provides for us day by day just as He did for the Israelites as they wandered through the wilderness. Every morning they would get up and go outside of their tents to find the manna that the Lord had provided for them. Day by day. They couldn't stock it up, but had to trust God to provide daily. That's why we pray, *"Give us this day our daily bread."*

I used to always worry about money and where it would come from, but now I know that God is the supplier and the giver of good gifts.

I recall the time that our bank account had hit a record low. We needed $200 to finish paying our monthly bills and there was no solution that I could see There were no resources that hadn't been tapped, but there was the heavenly storehouse and a generous Father.

So I went to the Source. "Father, it says in your word, *'Whatever things that I desire, when I pray if I believe that I receive them, then I shall have them'* (Mark 11:24). Right now I need $200 to pay these bills, so I'm asking for them in prayer believing that I will receive. Thank You, Lord."

I breathed a sigh of relief and decided to add a few more words to my prayer. "I really do thank You, Lord. This is a big load off of my mind knowing that I don't have to spend any more time worrying about these bills. Thanks again for taking care of everything."

A real peace came over me and I knew that the money would be coming soon. I truly believed in my heart that God was going to supply this need before the due date of the bills.

As I swept the rug that morning, I found myself wondering how God was going to work this financial miracle. Would there be another surprise check from my mother? Would we win the Reader's Digest Sweepstakes? I sang as I pushed the vacuum around the house. There was no reason to worry anymore. God was in the process of taking care of everything.

The dog started barking, signaling that the mailman was on his way up the front walk. As I removed the mail from the box, my heart sank. In my hand I was holding two envelopes from our insurance company, both containing bills.

Immediately the thought came into my mind, "What is this? I'm already short $200 and now I have two more bills to pay."

I instantly rebuked that thought. "Oh no you don't, Satan. My Father has the $200 on the way to me and when it arrives there will be more than enough to cover these bills too. You're a liar."

I opened the two bills, which totaled $68, and then I happened to look at the statement that was included with each one. There was an accounting of accumulated dividends for each policy and together the dividends added up to $268. There was $200 to cover our previous bills, as well as an additional $68 to pay for the insurance. Everything was covered down to the very last penny.

All that was necessary was a telephone call to the insurance agent requesting that the dividends be sent to us. Best of all, there was an opportunity to witness to the agent about the goodness of the Lord.

Another time there was a frantic knocking on my front door. I opened it to find a woman who often attended our Thursday night meeting standing there with tears running down her cheeks.

"I desperately need your help," she sobbed. "I don't know where else to turn. I just came from the electric company and they said that they're going to shut off my power today if I don't pay my bill by five o'clock. It's already four-thirty and I have no money. My welfare check isn't due until next week. Where am I going to get $127.50 in a half an hour?"

To be honest, I didn't know where she was going to get the money either, but I did know the God who could supply her need.

"Come in," I said taking her hand and drawing her inside. "We need to pray right now." Since we didn't have much time, I prayed a very quick prayer. I simply said, "Lord, help us!"

Keeping my eye on the clock, I rummaged through my purse and was able to find $55 in my wallet. There was another $20 bill folded up in a back pocket, and I discovered another $2.45 in loose change. I had run out of money and was quickly running out of time. Where was I going to get the rest of the money?

Suddenly, I heard another knock on the front door. This time it was a woman from my Bible study who was standing there.

"I feel really silly coming here to your house like this, but I have to ask you something. Do you need some money?"

Joy welled up within me as I nodded my head.

"Well, while I was driving home from the mall a few minutes ago, the Lord spoke to me and told me that I was to bring you some money." She reached into her jacket pocket and pulled out some bills. "He said this is what I am supposed to give you."

She handed me some folded bills. It was fifty dollars!

Doing a little accounting in my head, I asked her, "Do you have a nickel?" And of course, she did.

Needless to say, the electricity was never turned off. The bill was paid with about five minutes to spare before the company closed for the day. Don't ever hesitate to ask God for the things that you need. He delights in answering our prayers whether they are large or small.

I never minded when my children came to me and asked for a cookie or a hug. I was happy to help them tie their shoelaces or to read them a story because I loved them. I wanted to do things to make them happy and to give them things to make their lives more pleasant. This is all part of love and how the Lord delights in showing His love to us. It makes Him happy to make us happy. How I love the Lord. His mercy endures forever.

CHAPTER 13

HARVESTERS INTO THE FIELD

One of the greatest blessings is to be anointed by God to bring souls to salvation in Jesus Christ. What a thrill to be the instrument that the Lord is using to carry the gospel message into the world. In the past two years, Jack and I have prayed the salvation prayer with hundreds of people and had the privilege of seeing them born again.

There was Chuck, a Roman Catholic boy, who showed up at our Thursday evening meeting almost on a dare. He was a seeker who had tried just about everything before finally arriving at our house. As he came inside, Chuck looked Jack over very closely and then asked, "Are you a Reverend?" When he decided that my husband was "only an ordinary man," he decided to stay for the meeting.

Chuck must have liked what he experienced because a few days later we encountered him at another meeting about ten miles from our home. This time he seemed genuinely glad to see us and actually allowed us to share with him about Jesus and His love. Chuck was full of questions and also full of doubts, but he listened carefully to everything that we said.

"How do you know these things?" he asked Jack. "Did you go to Bible school?"

"No, I never attended Bible school or seminary," Jack replied. "I know about God because God is my Father."

Chuck shook his head in disbelief. "That's ridiculous. How can God possibly be your Father?"

"God became my Father when I believed that Jesus died for my sins," Jack explained. "I was born again and became a child of God. It happens when you believe."

"That's too easy," Chuck said stubbornly. "There has to be more to it than that."

Jack slipped a small witness Bible into Chuck's shirt pocket. "Read this. It will give you all of the answers that you need."

The next day Chuck was back at our house. "I came to return the little booklet you gave me last night. I don't take anything from anyone!"

Chuck's problem was made very clear to us. He didn't know how to receive. If Chuck couldn't receive the small gift that Jack had given him, how could he be expected to receive the free gift of forgiveness from God.

Jack and Chuck talked together for a long time about receiving God's love and the gift of salvation. "You have to reach out in faith, believing that the Lord wants you to be His child," Jack told him. "Believe and receive, doubt and do without. The decision is yours, Chuck. Before a gift can become yours, you have to receive it."

When he finally left our house that afternoon, Chuck carried away with him a book given to him by Jack.

"I want you to understand that I'm just borrowing this book," he stated. "I'm going to bring it back to you. I'm not going to keep it as a gift."

Chuck was still acting tough on the outside, but we knew that on the inside he was softening. The Holy Spirit was obviously ministering to Chuck's heart. It was just two weeks later when Chuck received the greatest gift known to man, the gift of salvation.

But that isn't the end of the story. It wasn't too much longer until Chuck received a glorious infilling of the Holy Spirit in a small Pentecostal church on a Sunday evening. For forty-five minutes Chuck couldn't even speak in English, but was praising the Lord in tongues. *"And they were all filled with the Holy Spirit and began to speak with other tongues as the Spirit gave them utterance"* (Acts 2:4). We were actually hesitant to let him drive home from the church because he was so "drunk on the new wine" of the spirit.

It's wonderful to look back and recall the many little lambs we have led into the flock of the Good Shepherd. There's a special story to tell about each one.

There was Viola, a Catholic woman, who appeared at our house one morning and announced, "They told me that if I came here, you would help me find Jesus."

She had attended a charismatic meeting a few months before at the invitation of a friend, and ever since that time she was aware that something was missing in her life. She was seeking the love, joy and peace that can only be found through Jesus. Viola was responding to the scripture that says, *"Seek and you shall find"* (Luke 9:11).

"I don't know what's wrong with me," she confessed. "I'm disgusted with myself, constantly in tears, mixed up in my thinking and wondering what life is all about."

"Viola," I asked, "if you were to die right now, do you know that you would go to heaven?"

This question has a profound effect on people, and I have found that it nearly always opens the door to present the gospel. There are other questions that can be asked, but sometimes they only gender confusion. "Are you saved?" means nothing to a person who isn't even aware that he is lost. "Have you been born again?" ninety-nine times out of a hundred will bring the response, "What are you talking about?"

But, the question, "If you were to die right now, do you know that you would go to heaven?" is guaranteed to bring a moment or two of deep reflection, and then a reply that reveals a person's standing with God.

I have heard many answers to that question. Some people think that they would get into heaven because they are a good person or a member of a certain church. Others think that they would be allowed in because they have kept most of the commandments. Some even claim that God allows everyone into heaven. All these answers are wrong.

There are also a few who honestly admit that they don't know if they would go to heaven or not. Many others are positive that the door to heaven would never open for them and readily acknowledge that they are sinners

What was Viola's answer? "I don't think I'd go to heaven," she responded. "I've done so many things in my life that were wrong. I know that I certainly don't deserve to go to heaven. I'll probably spend all eternity in purgatory trying to atone for my sins. No, if I died now, I definitely wouldn't go to heaven. God would never let me in."

"You can go to heaven," I assured her. "God loves you and He wants you to be happy here on earth, as well as to spend eternity with Him in heaven when you die."

Viola looked at me with tears in her eyes. "Do you really think so?"

"I don't just think so, but I know so," I replied. "You're miserable and unhappy because sin has separated you from God. It says in the Bible that *'All have sinned and come short of the glory of God'* (Romans 3:23). And it also says in the scriptures that *'The wages of sin is death'* (Romans 6:23). What those verses mean is that because you have sinned, you are spiritually dead and separated from God. Because of your sin, you can't really know God. You can know about Him, but you can't know Him personally."

"What shall I do?" Viola asked me.

Her heart was ready to receive the good news. "Believe that Jesus is your Savior and ask Him to come into your heart," I told her. "God loves us so much that He sent Jesus to die in our place. We are the ones who deserve to die, but Jesus became our substitute."

I reached out and took Viola's hands in mine. "When you receive Jesus as your Savior, the blood He shed on the cross washes away your sin and you can come into the presence of God. All you have to do is ask Jesus to forgive your sins and come into your heart."

Viola smiled, "Is that all there is to it?"

"All you have to do is believe. Have you ever wished that you could start all over again with your life? You can. When you receive Jesus into your heart, you are born again and you have a new beginning."

"That's what I want," Viola stated positively.

The Lord was ready to receive her into His kingdom. "Let's pray right now. You just repeat these words after me."

I put my arms around her and we bowed our heads. Without hesitation Viola prayed the simple words that would bring her salvation.

"Lord Jesus, I've sinned so many times and I'm sorry for all my sins. Please forgive me. I believe that You died on the cross for my sins and that You are my Savior. Come into my heart and make me the person You want me to be. Thank You, Jesus."

Tears flowed freely from both of us as Jesus came into her heart and she was cleansed. "I feel wonderful," Viola said. "I know something happened inside of me and it's just wonderful."

"The Lord has another gift for you," I told her. "He wants to give you the power of the Holy Spirit so you can live a victorious life in Christ Jesus."

"I certainly want everything that there is," Viola answered in faith. "If Jesus has something more for me, I want to receive it."

Gently laying my hands upon her, I prayed that the Lord would fill Viola to overflowing with His precious Holy Spirit.

Upon her face came the look of an angel and she began to speak, "Abba! Abba!" Heavenly words began to pour forth from her lips as she praised her newly found Lord and Savior.

How uncomplicated it is to receive salvation and the Lord's blessings. There is nothing you can do to bring it about except to believe that Jesus has already done it all for you. You don't have to understand how the new birth works. I don't understand how my television set works, but I have enough faith to push the button and turn it on. We must have the faith of a child, asking no questions, simply trusting in God. *"Whosoever shall not receive the kingdom of God as a little child shall in no wise enter therein"* (Luke 18:17).

With the faith of a child, Viola entered into the kingdom of God. She was saved and filled with the Holy Spirit within fifteen minutes after she knocked on our front door. She is now a completely new person, showing forth the love of God and leading others to Jesus.

God is ready to meet you anytime, anywhere. *"Today if you will hear His voice, harden not your hearts"* (Hebrews 4:7). It doesn't matter who you are or where you are. The Lord is ready to come into your heart if you are willing to open yourself and receive Him.

So many people think that they have to become "good enough" to be saved. You are never going to be good enough to be saved. It's impossible to stop sinning under your own power because of your old sinful nature. That's why you must be born again. It's a matter of recognizing your inability to save yourself and allowing Jesus to do it for you. *"God be merciful to me, a sinner"* (Luke 18:13). We can't earn our way into heaven. We have to come by the way of the cross. That's the only way. You must come through the blood of Jesus.

The Lord spoke to me one day while I was making the bed and said, *"Jean, I want you to go and pray with Marie Mills because I want her to receive My Son as her Savior today."*

Someday I will learn not to debate with God, but I haven't yet. "Father, Marie is ninety years old and living with her daughter-in-law. I just don't see how I can casually walk in and tell her that she needs to be saved."

No answer from the Lord. I debate with Him, but He doesn't debate with me. As far as God is concerned, there is no argument. Once He has told me something, He doesn't want to tell me again. The Lord expects me to be obedient without any argument. Delayed obedience is disobedience.

"Okay, Lord, You win. I'll go to visit Marie."

I stopped by a Christian bookstore on my way to her house to pick up a large print Bible. It was a perfect excuse to stop by to see Marie and would provide me with a golden opportunity to share the salvation message. Of course, I didn't need to worry about anything because the Holy Spirit had been there before me and already paved the way.

Within five minutes after my arrival, Marie's daughter-in-law left to go shopping, leaving Marie and me alone to discuss the spiritual things of life. Her heart was so ready to receive the eternal truths that lead to everlasting life. Marie told me how much she wanted to go to heaven, but that she never really understood what she had to do to assure her salvation.

How simple is the message: *"Believe on the Lord Jesus Christ and you shall be saved"* (Acts 16:31).

So many people say that they don't have enough faith to believe, but faith is a gift of God and comes by hearing the Word of God. What a beautiful scripture verse this is: *"Faith comes by hearing and hearing by the word of God"* (Romans 10:17). If you don't have enough faith, then start reading the Bible and allow the Word of God to be implanted in your heart.

That day Marie heard the word and she understood the wonderful truth that all she had to do was just believe. She reached out in faith and received the Lord Jesus into her heart. A brand new child of God was born in her ninetieth year on earth.

You are never too old or too young to accept Jesus as your Savior. He stands at the door of your heart and knocks and all you have to do is open your heart and receive Him. Through this simple act of faith, you become a new creature as God indwells you and takes over your life.

What a joy it is to serve the Lord and to share the wonderful message of salvation with others. When Jesus walked on earth, He told His disciples that the fields were white for the harvest. The fields are still white for the harvest today. I'm so glad that God not only called me to sow the seed, but also to help Him bring in the harvest.

CHAPTER 14

WE ARE A ROYAL PRIESTHOOD

As laymen, God leads us into some interesting situations with ordained ministers and priests. Many people cannot understand where Spirit-filled believers receive the authority to go out and preach the gospel, pray for the sick, cast out demons, and even baptize in a handy swimming pool. They feel that only those with degrees in theology should be doing such things.

"Where did Peter, James and John get their degrees?" I always ask. "What seminary did they attend?"

I have known many ordained ministers who have no personal knowledge of Jesus. Openly they will admit that they do not believe in the Bible as the true and inspired Word of God, the virgin birth, the physical resurrection of Jesus or His deity. They go forth in the name of Jesus, preaching another Jesus, another Spirit and another gospel.

You can have all the degrees known to man and yet not know Jesus. You can be able to read the Bible in Latin, Hebrew and Greek and not know Jesus. The mightiest church leaders can lay hands upon you for confirmation and ordination, but if you don't know Jesus it is for naught.

Jesus has given authority to His disciples, to those who recognize Him as Savior and Lord. The Pharisees were the religious leaders when Jesus walked on earth, yet they didn't recognize Him as the Son of God, come in the flesh. Titles, fancy robes, degrees in theology and long prayers do not make you a disciple. It is only the Holy Spirit dwelling in your heart who can anoint you to be a disciple.

The Lord has a special concern for ministers and priests who are serving as leaders in the churches today. God wants the unsaved to be born again and the saved to enter into the fullness of the Spirit. And often He will use a simple little disciple to deliver His message to them.

We were attending a breakfast meeting at a convention in Washington and found ourselves sitting next to a distinguished white-haired gentleman from West Virginia. Conversation revealed that he was a Baptist minister.

"Have you received the Holy Sprit since you first believed?" Jack asked him, aware that many pastors are not aware of the second blessing.

What a wonderful gift the Holy Spirit is. The Lord has sent Him from heaven to dwell within us, to comfort us and to empower us to witness for His glory. Maybe you don't need the baptism of the Spirit to get into heaven, but I personally wouldn't want to go across the street without His indwelling power. A Christian living without the power of the Holy Spirit is like someone trying to drive a car that has no gas. *"Be not drunk with wine, wherein is excess, but be filled with the Spirit"* (Ephesians 5:18).

When you are baptized in the Holy Spirit, the Bible becomes a modern textbook for use today. When I read the book of Acts, I read about people just like me and my friends. The many letters that the Apostle Paul wrote to the churches were written to Spirit-filled believers, and I can relate to them today without any difficulty.

I once heard a Catholic priest relate that before he received the baptism of the Spirit, he could preach on the four gospels without any difficulty. But when he attempted to preach on the Book of Acts and the epistles, he was at a loss as to the meaning they conveyed.

When you are baptized in the Spirit, the gifts become a daily manifestation in your life. You don't have to ponder the meaning of verses describing them, because you know from personal experience that the spiritual gifts are for today. God doesn't only call people to be disciples, but He equips them with spiritual gifts as well.

The Baptist minister listened intently as Jack related how he had experienced his own Pentecost and become a bold witness for Jesus Christ. Following the close of the meeting, we had the privilege of praying for the minister and his wife, and rejoiced with them as they received the baptism of the Spirit with the evidence of speaking in tongues.

About six months later we met him again at a meeting where we were speaking in West Virginia. As a matter of fact, he was even the one who introduced us. I will never forget what he said: "I praise God that I had breakfast last winter with a Presbyterian layman who had the boldness to ask an ordained Baptist minister if he had received the Holy Spirit since he first believed."

There are times when the Lord asks us to share with someone and it is a very difficult assignment to carry out. One such experience had to do with a Roman Catholic priest.

I was standing in the bathroom rolling up my hair one morning (it's funny where God will speak to you), and the Lord said to me, *"Jean, I want you to go to the Catholic church and pray for the priest."*

I was stunned when I heard what the Lord expected me to do. "Father, I can't do that. The priest will think that I'm some kind of a crazy woman. After all, he's a Catholic priest and I'm a suburban housewife. What's he going to think if I just show up on his doorstep and say that You sent me to pray for him? He'll call for the men with the white coats. I just can't do this, Lord."

Self dies hard. We are so concerned with what people think about us. Even though I know that I have been crucified with Christ, and even though I reckon myself dead, that "old man" keeps trying to come up out of the grave to haunt me. How patient God is with me.

"Jean, I told you that I want you to go to the Catholic church and pray for the priest. Where is your faith?"

"I'm sorry, Lord, but I'm just not going to do it."

The rest of the morning I walked around with verses like these running through my mind: *"If you love Me, keep My commandments"* (John 14:15). *"Rebellion is as the sin of witchcraft and stubbornness is as iniquity and idolatry"* (I Samuel 15:23).

I went to the grocery store, strongly aware of the presence of the Lord and of my disobedience. The love, joy and peace that normally filled my heart had been displaced by a spirit of heaviness. I was experiencing what Jonah must have felt when he told the Lord he wasn't going to Nineveh. I didn't like the feeling at all.

Finally I gave in. *"Forgive me, Father. If You want me to go, then I'll go. I'm willing to make a fool of myself for You, Jesus. Just let me check out of the store and I'll go right on over to the church."*

It was a real relief to be back in right standing with the Lord. Love, joy and peace once more flooded my being. *"If we confess our sin, He is faithful and just to forgive us our sin and to cleanse us from all unrighteousness"* (I John 1:9).

I set a new record getting through the checkout line, and then I was on my way over to the Catholic church. I must admit that my heart was beating double time as I pulled into the parking lot. I got out of the car and walked over to the rectory and rang the doorbell.

No answer. I rang again. Still no answer. "Praise the Lord," I thought, "he's not home." I turned and started down the steps, when the door opened and the housekeeper was standing there.

"If you're looking for the priest, he isn't here," she informed me. "He's out making house calls and probably won't be back for another hour or two. Do you want to leave a message?"

"No, that's all right," I replied with relief. I was surprised at this turn of events. Why would God send me to see someone who wasn't there? But I felt as though I had been given a reprieve and I wasn't going to argue about it. Perhaps all God wanted was for me to be willing to obey Him.

As I headed back to my car, out of the corner of my eye, I happened to notice a car coming down the street toward the church. In the car was a man wearing a black shirt and jacket with a white collar. Could it possibly be? The car turned into the parking lot and pulled in beside mine. Before I really had time to digest what was happening, the priest and I were standing face to face.

I took a deep breath and plunged in. "My name is Jean Coleman and the Lord told me to come and pray for you."

He looked at me puzzled for a few moments and finally replied, "That's very nice, but as a rule, I usually do my own praying."

"Well, that's up to you," I answered. "All I know is what the Lord told me to do. I'm just here because He told me to come and pray for you."

The priest looked me over as he considered my request. "Don't get me wrong," he finally stated. "I'm always happy when someone really wants to pray for me."

I held out my hands. "I'll pray for you right now if you will allow me." He placed his hands in mine and standing in the parking lot, we bowed our heads together and I prayed.

"Father, bless this man that You have called to be a shepherd of this flock. Give him wisdom and knowledge to guide Your people in the paths of righteousness. Grant him power to overcome the doubts and fears that come upon him and fill him with Your peace and love. In Jesus' name. Amen."

That may not have been the exact prayer, but it was along those lines. It wasn't a prayer that was terribly inspired or earth shattering. There was no mighty revelation. It was just a prayer marking a lesson in obedience for me, and I suspect, an act of humility for the priest.

"Thank you, Jean," the priest said withdrawing his hand from mine.

"May God bless you in your ministry," I replied.

The priest turned and went into the rectory and I got into my car. God's perfect timing. Just two or three minutes spent together in a parking lot praying together. There were no extra words or idle talk. It was just God's will being carried out in faith and obedience.

It's so beautiful the way the Lord brings His people together. There is no such thing as an accidental meeting in the life of a Christian. When I meet someone at the store, I know that God has brought us together. If I sit next to someone at a meeting, I believe that the Lord has arranged it. If we go out to eat, I believe our waiter or waitress has been chosen by God. I recognize that I am led by His Spirit, so I keep my eyes and ears open to take advantage of any opportunities He gives me to serve Him and share His love with others.

God uses ordinary people to do His will. We are His ministers even though we don't wear collars or have our names preceded by the title of "Reverend." The Bible states that we are *"a chosen generation, a royal priesthood, a holy nation, a peculiar people"* (I Peter 2:6), and that's good enough for me.

CHAPTER 15

SIGNS AND WONDERS FOLLOWING

The Bible says that *"Signs shall follow those that believe"* (Mark 16:17). To have something follow you, it is necessary to keep moving forward. When you are standing still in unbelief, nothing will ever be able to follow after you.

I truly believe that the same power that flowed through the early disciples still flows through Spirit-filled disciples today. We should be experiencing the same signs and wonders in our lives that are described in the New Testament.

I have searched the scriptures and never found any place where it says that miracles have ceased. Nor have I found a verse that even suggests that the power working through me is any different from the power in the original disciples. What hinders the working of miracles today is our lack of faith. We are the body of Christ, and the Lord wants to use us as His mouth, His hands and His feet. To think that God works through ordinary people staggers the imagination.

One morning we were in church when an elderly woman stood up and requested prayer. She had recently been to an eye doctor about her failing vision. Her physician had run many tests and finally told her that there was nothing more that medical science could do. Her eyesight was gone and there was no reason for her to return for further treatment.

The woman's voice cracked as she told the congregation, "I really can't see anything at all now. I have been declared legally blind."

Together we raised our voices in prayer asking the Lord to intercede on her behalf. The service continued, but my mind was only on the plight of this woman. When church ended, nothing could have kept me away from her side. I was filled with faith that her eyes could be healed.

"May I pray for you?" I asked.

"That would be very nice."

"Do you believe that God is able to heal your eyes today?"

"Yes, I do."

Gently I placed my thumbs over her eyes. "Be healed in the name of Jesus of Nazareth. Open your eyes and see clearly."

There was no feeling of power or a great surge of faith. I just moved in obedience to the leading of the Lord and spoke aloud a few simple words.

I removed my fingers from her eyes and she slowly opened them.

"My God!" she shouted. "I can see! I can see faces!" She slowly turned, looking toward the front of the church. "Oh, look! I can see the cross there on the wall! I can see! I can see again!"

She suddenly ran across the church to where the pastor was standing and threw her arms around him. "Praise Jesus! I can see!"

Jack and I slipped quietly out the back door. I don't think she ever knew who it was that had prayed for her. And it didn't really matter. What mattered was that she was healed.

No, the age of miracles has not passed away. God is still saving, healing, baptizing and delivering.

Once we received a phone call from a woman saying that she was very ill and needed us to come over and pray for her. When we got to her apartment, we found her lying on the couch. Her eyes were rolled back in her head and there was no sign of life. We immediately rebuked the spirit of death, claimed the life-giving power of the Holy Spirit in her body and began mouth-to-mouth resuscitation. By the time the rescue squad arrived, she was breathing again. God had us in the right place at the right time.

What constitutes a miracle? Certainly changed lives, teens delivered from drugs and adults from alcohol, people who were once miserable and unhappy now rejoicing in the Lord, bodies healed, marriages restored and prayers answered must all be counted as miracles. The list is endless. God is still a miracle-working God, for those who have the eyes to see.

Why is the world so blind to the mighty acts of God? I ask myself this question often. Yet I know the answer from my own experience because there was a time when I walked the earth completely blind to the kingdom of God. My spiritual eyes were unseeing. The Bible says, *"Except a man is born again, he cannot see the kingdom of God"* (John 3:3).

Then one day Jesus passed by and He touched me. Suddenly my spiritual eyes were opened and I could see. But although the kingdom of God surrounded me, I still couldn't really comprehend the things of God.

There was a blind man in Bethsaida who had the same problem. His eyes had been opened when Jesus first touched him, but he looked around and said, *"I see men, but I can't see them very clearly. They look like trees walking"* (Mark 8:24). The Bible tells us that Jesus put His hands once again upon the man's eyes and his sight was completely restored and he saw every man clearly.

I thank Jesus for His second touch upon my life. The baptism of the Holy Spirit gave me the ability to see clearly the things of God without the distortion caused by church doctrines and preconceived ideas. The scriptures were opened to me in a way I never thought was possible. The reality of the kingdom of God unfolded before me.

The world needs to have its spiritual eyes opened. So many people are wandering around in darkness, not even knowing they are blind. If you are in darkness and are totally blind, you don't even know if there is a light shining. The world needs those who will bring the message that the Light has come and that Jesus is the Light.

Let me tell you about a fifteen-year old boy named James who came into our lives and had an encounter with the God of miracles. Early one morning there was a knock at our front door and standing on the front porch was our good friend, Bob, and at his side was the dirtiest boy I had ever seen in my entire life.

"Jean, this is James and I brought him here for some breakfast," Bob informed me.

It seems that Bob had been driving to work and noticed James at the side of the road hitch-hiking. The Lord told Bob to stop his car, pick James up and bring him over to our house. The boy eagerly accepted the ride.

As they rode along together, James explained that two weeks earlier he had left his home in Texas to escape an alcoholic stepfather. He had been traveling to Florida with two other boys in their aged car when it had come to an abrupt halt, apparently never to run again. They had simply abandoned the car and continued their journey on foot.

It didn't take the boys long to realize that the three of them were never going to thumb down a ride together, so they split up, agreeing that they would meet in New Orleans two days later. When James finally arrived at their designated meeting place, his friends were nowhere to be found. He waited and waited, but they never showed up. Fortunately, James met a young couple who allowed him to stay in their apartment for a few days.

During his stay they gave him a small booklet called "The Four Spiritual Laws." God was obviously preparing James' heart for what awaited him further down the road.

Soon it became obvious to James that his friends were never coming, and he was faced with two choices. One, he could go back home to Texas and the deplorable situation there. Or two, he could travel up to Delaware where he had a married sister. James made the decision to head north.

He was heading to Delaware when Bob picked him up in Maryland along the highway. James was flat broke. His pockets held only a road map of the east coast and the tract that he been given in New Orleans. James hadn't eaten for three days, and the night before he had slept by the side of the road with the rain beating down upon him. Traveling in the clothes he was wearing, he had nothing with him but an extra T-shirt. His underwear and socks hadn't been changed in weeks and his feet were covered with blisters.

Talk about eating! James ate a breakfast that would have satisfied a family of four. Since Bob was on his way to work, he gave James to me for safekeeping during the day. It was my morning to teach a Bible study, so I left James at the kitchen table, suggesting he take a nap on the couch until I got back. I had to believe that this young man wasn't a thief and that the Lord would watch over my home and possessions.

The Bible study turned into a prayer meeting for James and an offering was received to buy him some new clothes. Two of the women Dorothy and Adele, came home with me after the meeting, greeting James with big hugs. While I went out to pick up some hamburgers for our lunch, they proceeded to tell James about how much he was loved by Jesus.

"God loves you and He has a wonderful plan for your life," they assured him. "It's no accident that you're here right now in Laurel, Maryland. The Lord definitely has His hand upon you."

As the three of us ate lunch together, James related what had happened that morning just before Bob stopped to pick him up.

"It was really amazing," James said. "There I was standing by the road and I didn't know what was going to happen to me. My money was gone and I was really scared. So I just knelt down and prayed, asking God to help me. The next thing I knew, Bob was pulling over and asking me if I wanted a ride."

James shared with us about his problems at home, the lack of love and understanding, a stepfather who abused his mother and the entire family, a life void of meaning. He loved his sister who lived in Delaware and was confident that she would open her home to him when he got there.

However, there was a great difficulty. All James knew was that his sister lived in Delaware. He didn't know the name of the city where she was living or even her husband's first name. He was traveling only with the information that Marian Abraham lived somewhere in the state of Delaware.

"I'll be able to find her," James said confidently. "Delaware is a small state and there aren't too many cities and towns there. I'll just travel around from town to town until I locate her." How beautiful is the faith of a child.

We sent James off for a shower and another nap while the three of us discussed the situation. What do you do with a runaway boy who doesn't even know where he's heading and won't give a clue as to where he came from in Texas? Sometimes all you can do is pray.

Around five o'clock Jack came home from work, took off his coat, loosened his tie, and put his arm around James saying, "Let me tell you about a friend of mine named Jesus."

Fifteen minutes later, James had a friend named Jesus too. Not only did he have a friend, but also a Savior. James was no longer a lost runaway boy. He had been found by the Good Shepherd and added to His flock.

James also had another friend named Dorothy, who had not only been praying for him but also making some inquiries on his behalf. Only a few minutes after James received Jesus, Dorothy burst in the front door with some amazing news.

"James, I just finished talking with your sister on the phone and she wants you to come and live with her."

I could hardly believe my ears. "Praise the Lord!" I shouted. "How did you reach her? All you knew was her name. I can hardly believe this has happened." Why are we always so astonished when our prayers are answered?

Dorothy explained to us what had taken place. "I called a long distance operator and told her I wanted to reach a Mrs. Abraham in Delaware. Of course, she told me that it was impossible to locate someone without having a full name and the name of their city."

But Dorothy knew that with God all things are possible so she didn't get discouraged or give up.

"I just told the operator all about James and how the Lord wanted him to find his sister. So she put me through to her supervisor, who then talked to some other people there in her office. Finally they agreed to place a call to every number in the state of Delaware under the name Abraham, inquiring if anyone in the household had a fifteen-year-old brother named James who lived in Texas."

Dorothy was practically bouncing with excitement as she finished telling her miracle. "Would you believe that after only making three calls, they were in touch with James' sister? She knew he had left home and was really worried about him. Mirian can't wait to have James with her in Delaware, so he has a new home waiting there for him."

How great is our God! The next morning found James, dressed in clean clothes and carrying a small suitcase containing a whole new wardrobe, boarding a bus to Wilmington. He had a Bible in his hand and twenty dollars in his pocket.

Arrangements had been made with a Christian man to meet the bus and drive him to his sister's house that was located only about ten miles from Wilmington.

No little lamb is too small, too unimportant or too lost, to be of concern to the Father. He hears the heart cry of the lost and through His people on earth, the Lord ministers His love. We thank God for allowing us to be a part of James' miracle. How beautifully God weaves together the members of the body of Christ to accomplish His will. A couple in New Orleans sheltered James, Bob found him on the highway, I fed him, Jack led him to Jesus, Dorothy located his sister, the women in the Bible study clothed him and an unknown brother in Delaware delivered him to his new home. What a tremendous example of God's people working together in unity under the direction of the Holy Spirit, each one doing his little part to make up the whole.

We never saw James again, but we know that he is in God's care. When you are willing to be used, the Lord will use you. And when you have finished one task, He will move you on to another. There's always another miracle waiting just around the corner.

CHAPTER 16

WHO'S SPEAKING?

One of the biggest problems that Christians seem to have is that they are unable to distinguish the voice of God. "I've never heard God speak to me," they often say. However, the difficulty is not that they didn't hear Him, but that they didn't recognize His voice when He spoke.

It is important to know that you can hear three voices. <u>First</u>, there is the voice of God. His voice is small and still, and if you have a lot of worry, fear, prejudice, hate, bitterness and unbelief crashing around within your mind, it is almost impossible to hear God quietly speaking. *"Be still and know that I am God,"* (Psalm 46:10), the Lord commands. We need to quiet ourselves and then we can hear the Lord speak within our heart.

The Lord is continually speaking these words to me, *"Relax. Rest in Me and let not your heart be troubled."* As a type A personality, I am always on the go and my mind is continually filled with a list of things to do. I have learned that if I really want to hear God's voice, I need to "come apart before I come apart." My greatest need is to quiet myself and listen in the stillness of my heart.

As believers, we all need to cast all our troubles and problems aside and come into His presence. Not only do we live in a sound-filled world where the television or radio is always blaring, but our minds are filled with a barrage of noisy thoughts. How can we possibly expect to hear the Lord in the midst of all that clamor? We need to learn to rest in the Lord as a baby rests in the arms of his mother. That's when we can really experience the peace that passes all understanding and hear the voice of God in the depths of our hearts.

When God speaks, He will never contradict His Word. If the voice you are hearing is truly God, it will always agree with what is written in the scriptures. And the Lord never bullies, shoves, pushes or compels. He gently leads and encourages you to follow. Jesus said, *"My sheep hear My voice and I know them, and they follow Me"* (John 10:27).

God speaks to us from within, where we can hear His voice in our spirits. But the Lord can also speak through other people, and then we can hear His voice through our natural ears.

Be sure to listen carefully to the sermon that is preached in your church on a Sunday morning. The Lord always has a special word tucked away in every message for those who have the ears to hear. You can be sure that God's word never returns void.

Many times God has spoken to me through the lips of my husband to bring me encouragement and wise counsel. But, of course, there are other times the Lord will use Jack to bring a word of correction or even rebuke. I don't always appreciate correction from Jack, but I have come to recognize that he is simply serving as a messenger passing on a word from God.

Wives, listen to your husbands. God speaks to you through them all the time. God can use their lips, and you will sense the witness of the Holy Spirit within you say, *"That's Me you hear speaking, so pay attention."*

The most common way that God speaks to His people is through the Bible. It's amazing how often I can hear God's voice speaking to me directly from the pages of His Word. I'll just be reading along in the scriptures when suddenly a verse will leap out at me and I know in my heart that it's a direct word from the Lord.

But beware of spiritual roulette. Many people play this dangerous game. "Do you have a word for me today, Lord?" And then the Bible is opened, a finger placed on the page and the message read. In spiritual roulette your "spin" could bring up something like this: "Thus saith the Lord, Behold, I will bring evil upon this place and upon the inhabitants thereof." That's a random verse from the Bible found in II Chronicles 24:24.

What do you do with a message like that? Ask the Lord for another verse?

Does that sound like what our Heavenly Father would say to His child? Remember, not every verse in the Bible is addressed to you personally. It's one thing when the Bible speaks to you, and quite another when you *make* it speak to you. When Satan tempted Jesus in the wilderness, he used scripture to tempt Him. So be alert to Satan's tricks.

God can also speak through friends and neighbors, and even through strangers. He also will speak to you through brothers and sisters in the Lord, and don't forget that once, God even spoke through a donkey (Numbers 22:30). Be alert because God can speak to you through anyone.

The <u>second</u> voice that we can hear is the voice of the devil. Satan can speak in many ways. He usually tries to reach you in your mind, luring you away from the truth of God. Many times it is much easier to hear the devil's loud, harsh voice, than God's still small one. Never forget that Satan is a liar, a deceiver and a thief. He's out to steal your love, joy and peace.

Satan can also speak to you through people, just like the Lord does. If you think about it, you can surely remember being tempted to do wrong by someone you considered a friend. Sometimes the devil will even use the voice of someone you love to stir up a response from within you that isn't becoming to a believer. Satan knows your weak spots and will try to reach them through insults and criticism spoken through the mouths of friends and even family members.

One time Jesus began to tell His disciples that He had to go into Jerusalem and suffer many things and be killed. His disciple Peter actually rebuked Jesus saying, *"Oh no, Lord. This isn't going to happen to You."*

Jesus turned to Peter and rebuking him replied, *"Get thee behind Me, Satan"* (Matthew 16:23). The Lord recognized that the devil was speaking through Peter, tempting Him to turn away from the cross. Do not be deceived. Satan will try anything to turn you away from God's perfect will.

I've heard Satan speak through Jack, and I know that the devil has also spoken through me to others more times than I care to admit. This is why we need to bridle our tongues and guard the words of our mouth. *"Let every man be swift to hear, slow to speak and slow to anger"* (James 1:19).

There is yet a third voice that can be heard in our inner man. We can hear our own thoughts that are running through our minds. The Bible instructs us to *"bring into captivity every thought to the obedience of Christ"* (II Corinthians 10:5). My natural thoughts may present themselves as good ideas, but they are often worldly and unspiritual. Examine your thoughts to be sure that they are acceptable in the sight of the Lord.

What should we be thinking about? One day I took the words from Philippians 4:8 and paraphrased them into a little poem:

> Whatsoever things are honest,
> Whatsoever things are true,
> If they're just and pure and lovely,
> God has given them to you.
> If they're things of good report
> And if there's virtue, if there's praise,
> Think on these things,
> Think on these things all your days.

I refer to these wonderful words from scripture as God's prescription for peace. If you put these words into practice in your life, you will overcome worry and fear and walk in the peace that passes all understanding.

It always pays to know which voice you're hearing. Test the spirits. Is it the Holy Spirit, an evil spirit, or your own spirit? Learn to distinguish the difference. Use your spiritual gift of discernment.

You will find that as you continue to study the scriptures, God's voice will become so familiar that you'll never again have to ask, "Is that You, Lord?" You'll be able to recognize His voice because you know it so well.

Speak, Lord. Your servant hears.

CHAPTER 17

THE GIFTS OF THE SPIRIT

When you are baptized in the Holy Spirit, you will receive spiritual gifts. The Holy Spirit is <u>THE</u> gift, but when He comes, He brings spiritual gifts along with Him. These gifts are not for your own personal use, but rather to provide you a way to be a blessing to others. However, having the gifts is one thing, and using them is another.

Jack tells the story of a man who received a necktie as a Christmas gift. He expressed thanks to the giver of the gift and then put the tie on the top shelf of his closet. The tie was never worn and soon forgotten.

You can also receive gifts from God and never use them. To use the Christmas tie, you must make the effort to wrap it around your neck. If you receive an electric iron, you must plug it in. A gift cannot be enjoyed by anyone if it is just left in a box somewhere. It takes a definite action on the part of the receiver.

Peter and some of the other disciples were in a boat one day when they saw Jesus walking on the water. After being reassured that it was really the Lord, Peter cried out, "Lord, tell me to come over to You walking on the water." And Jesus replied saying, "All right. Come along over here."

The Bible tells us that when Peter heard the word of the Lord, he actually got out of the boat and walked across the water to go to Jesus (Matthew 14:28-29).

How I love that illustration, because it's a wonderful example of faith in action. Peter put feet under his faith. He actually got out of the boat and he walked on the water. That took great faith. Peter had never walked on the water before and he had never seen anyone else ever walk on the water before except for Jesus. But Peter remembered that Jesus had once said, *"These things that I do, you shall do also, and you will do even greater things than these"* (John 14:12).

Peter had heard Jesus speak to him and say, "Come." Peter didn't hesitate for even a minute. He obeyed and stepped out in faith.

Each of us has to do exactly what Peter did if we are going to walk in faith. We have to get out of the boat, and that isn't always easy. You have to put one foot upon the water and then the other. Then you have to do the hardest thing of all. You have to let go of the side of the boat and walk in faith in obedience to the word of the Lord.

I'll never forget the first time the Lord used me to give an interpretation of tongues. Jack and I were attending a service at a small Pentecostal church near our home, when suddenly someone on the other side of the sanctuary boldly spoke out in tongues. In the silence that followed, I became aware of five words repeating themselves over and over in my mind. I kept hearing, *"I have given a promise ..."*

I also sensed the Lord speaking in my heart and saying, *"I am giving you the interpretation and I want you to speak it aloud."*

Almost immediately Satan began to taunt me with words bringing doubt and fear. "How can you possibly give an interpretation with only five words? You know nothing about any promise. What if you say those five little words and nothing more is given to you?" The devil's voice spoke so loudly that I

114

could hear him clearly over my pounding heart. "You're going to look like some sort of fool. Why would God choose to use you anyway?"

The five little words continued running through my mind, *"I have given a promise . . ."*

I felt like my heart was attempting to set a new record for rapid beating. My mouth was dry and fear was grabbing hold of me with icy fingers that sent chills through me.

"Lord, I can't."

"Jean, you can do all things through Christ who strengthens you. I am here and I will give you strength. Get out of the boat."

I can sympathize with Peter because I know just how he must have felt when he moved out across the water in faith.

I opened my mouth and put one foot out of the boat.

"Father, I just can't do this."

"Yes you can. Have faith, My child."

"God help me."

"Just keep your eyes on Me and you won't sink. Start walking right now."

I took a deep breath and let go of the boat. In faith I opened my mouth and began to speak the words that the Lord had placed within me.

"I have given a promise to My people and I am not a man that I should lie." The words continued to flow from my mouth, without any effort on my part, as I yielded myself to God. I had stepped out in faith and the Lord was holding me up, giving me the words, filling my mouth.

I had walked on the water as surely as Peter had so long ago. And once the fear was behind me, I was filled with exhilaration.

"Thank You, Lord, for using me."

It's so hard to take that first step, but there always has to be a first step before you can take the second. The Lord requires that step of faith, if you are going to move across the water to Him.

You can have confidence that the Lord is right there with you, holding your hand to keep you afloat.

It is recorded that five times Jesus rebuked His disciples with these words, *"Oh you of little faith."* You can check out the verses for yourself in the Gospels of Matthew and Luke. Our constant prayer should be that the Lord will increase our faith. It is impossible to minister the spiritual gifts without faith. You must get out of the boat and walk across the water.

One afternoon I was at the post office waiting in line to buy some stamps. Clearly I heard the Lord speaking to me.

"Do you see that man standing in front of you? He has come to pick up a Bible that he has ordered, but the Bible is not yet here."

What an amazing revelation to receive so unexpectedly! I studied the young man and could see nothing unusual about him. But obviously God had given me this information for some reason.

Being prompted by the spirit, I reached into my purse and took out the small red Bible I always carried with me. It was time to get out of the boat. Tapping him on the shoulder, I stated, "The Bible you are expecting isn't here yet, but maybe you can read this in the meantime."

Slowly he turned to face me, and without hesitation accepted the little Bible I was offering to him. Then from his pocket, he removed a gospel tract which he handed to me.

Just at that moment the postal clerk returned to the counter and said, "I'm sorry, but your package hasn't yet arrived. The truck is a little late today, so we won't be getting the delivery until after three o'clock."

With a smile the man remarked to me, "I'm not sure how you knew, but I'm waiting for a new study Bible that I ordered the other day. I guess I'll be waiting a little longer." Extending his hand to me, he introduced himself. "I'm Don Thomas of Riverdale Baptist Church and it looks like the Lord has brought us together. Let's go outside and talk for a few minutes."

A few minutes turned into thirty minutes as we shared about Jesus and how He had changed our lives. Don had been reading about the charismatic movement and was leery about the whole idea of a second experience, especially about speaking in tongues. He had been curious to meet someone who was claiming to have received the baptism of the Holy Spirit. God had opened the door for a hungry seeker to hear firsthand about the fullness of the Spirit and the spiritual gifts.

I never saw Don again, but I did mail him some literature on the baptism of the Spirit. God had brought us together in response to a seeking heart, and through the gift of a word of knowledge, contact was made. We need to listen to the inner guidance of the Spirit as He speaks to us in that still, small voice. But listening is not enough. When we hear, we must move out in faith and carry out His wishes.

When I received the Holy Spirit, I received the spiritual gifts as well. They are all within me, waiting for God to release them as the need arises. If I am making a hospital visit, I don't need the gift of interpretation of tongues. I need the gift of healing, faith or miracles. The gifts have already been provided, and are just awaiting the time of their manifestation.

As a Bible teacher, the Lord has often granted me the word of wisdom. He will inspire me to tell a very simple parable or story, yet it will be an illustration containing such truth that lives are forever changed. Many times as Jack and I have ministered together in meetings, God has given us the word of knowledge regarding a healing that has taken place.

So often it is our lack of faith that hinders the moving of the Spirit. Once the two of us were the speakers at a gathering in Virginia. After an extended period of worship, a silence fell upon the gathering and everyone there waited expectantly to hear a word of prophecy from the Lord.

Nothing. Only silence. Everyone continued to wait. And finally, into my innermost being, came the words, *"The time has come, My children . . ."*

I hesitated to speak forth the prophecy. It was like I was frozen in time. The silence continued and still I didn't speak. How the Lord must despair over my stubborn spirit.

"Lord," I pleaded, "please give the prophecy to someone else tonight. We just finished sharing a long message and I'm spiritually drained."

Yet, even as I thought those words, I felt conviction and had a change of heart. How could I possibly refuse to obey God?

But it was too late! The silence ended and everyone began to sing.

Later, when we were back in our hotel room, I confessed to Jack that I had received a word of prophecy, but hadn't given it.

Jack laughed. "I have news for you. That wasn't a prophecy that you received. It was an interpretation of tongues. The Lord gave me a message in tongues at that time and I didn't yield to His will either. I didn't give it."

It's nice to know that Jack is as human as I am and that sometimes even my husband has trouble getting out of the boat. How wonderful it is to know that God understands this. He opens wide His big Father's heart and embraces us just the way we are, loving us in spite of all our many faults and shortcomings.

Lord, minister the gifts through me. And if I don't get out of the boat, please give me a push! I want to walk on the water with You.

CHAPTER 18

THE FRUIT OF THE SPIRIT

One cannot talk about the spiritual gifts without discussing the fruit of the Spirit. As trees of righteousness, our purpose is to bear fruit for the glory of God. The spiritual gifts are like the leaves on the tree, and the spiritual fruit can be compared to a bountiful harvest of big red juicy apples. A healthy productive tree needs to have both.

Here is the spiritual fruit (note that the word is singular not plural) that every tree should be bearing: love, joy, peace, patience, gentleness, goodness, faith, meekness, and self-control (Galatians 5:22). All Christians should be bringing forth this fruit in their lives, and if they don't, something is very wrong.

Love seems to be the first fruit to come forth after you receive Jesus as your Savior. I bubbled over with love as a new Christian, and I pray that I still do today. I would walk through the aisles of the grocery store and bite my tongue to keep from shouting out, "Listen, everybody! I want you to know that I love you!" I had learned to view people through the eyes of God. I had been given the eyes to see their potential and their need. I was filled to overflowing with love, and the God kind of love is something that must be shared with others.

I learned to look on the inside of people to see their hearts and not to judge by their outward appearance. People were transformed before my eyes into little lost lambs in need of a shepherd. I was overcome with compassion as I saw the suffering, misery and loneliness that abounds on the earth. People without the Lord are on the path to death and destruction.

The world's greatest treasure was mine and I wanted to share Jesus and His love with everyone. Love is God's greatest gift and I had His love dwelling within my humble frame. It was too wonderful to keep to myself. I wanted everyone to become a partaker of His great love.

I had become aware of these wonderful, transforming verses: *"Let this mind be in you which was also in Christ Jesus"* (Philippians 2:5). *"For who has known the mind of the Lord that he may instruct Him? But we have the mind of Christ"* (I Corinthians 2:16). *"Be not conformed to this world: but be ye transformed by the renewing of your mind that you may prove what is that good and acceptable and perfect will of God"* (Romans 12:2).

When I first came into the presence of the Lord, His mind and my mind were a thousand miles apart. God's thoughts were certainly not my thoughts and His ways were not my ways, and then I read in the Word that I should let the mind of Christ dwell in me. I needed to learn to think like Jesus, to think His thoughts. My mind needed to be renewed.

First, I became acquainted with Jesus through reading the Bible, especially the Gospels. How did Jesus react to situations, people, temptation? I needed to know so that I could react the same way.

The beautiful thing is that Jesus is *"the same yesterday, today and forever"* (Hebrews 13:8). He doesn't change because of a hard day at the office or a bad headache. Jesus is also not a respecter of persons. He is completely free of prejudices. What He does for one, He will do for all.

As time passed, I came to know Jesus better than I even knew Jack. "What would Jesus do?" I would ask myself a hundred times a day. And if I didn't know, I would search the scriptures to find the answer. Before long, I found that I was responding just like Jesus would have done. My mind was truly being changed. I was being renewed in the spirit of my mind. Two minds were merging into one. What an amazing miracle!

My walk in the Lord revolves around these three questions: What would Jesus do? What would Jesus say? How would Jesus react in this same situation? We need to ask, "What would You do, Jesus?" Then whatever He says to you, do it. You can know the will of God for your life.

It isn't always easy to demonstrate the love of Jesus. God placed in my care several very unlovable people, and then instructed me on how to love them with the love of the Lord. I learned to look beneath the hard, cold exteriors and see the lost confused children crying out from within them. I learned to hate the sin, but to love the sinner. Many times I would pray, "Lord, I can't love this unlovable person." Then I would hear His still, small voice reply, *"Love her through Me."*

How faithful the Lord is to give grace upon grace. When I feel like I am running out of love, I only have to recall how much God loves me, and if the Lord loves me so much, how can I not share that love with others? His grace is always sufficient.

Growing the fruit of the spirit takes patience. Fruit doesn't grow overnight. It can be a long, slow process. The tree has to put down its roots and become firmly planted. Then eventually the blossoms appear, the promise of fruit to come. Slowly day by day the fruit grows, increasing in size. So it is with the fruit of the spirit.

Although every fruit of the spirit should be displayed through a believer's life, sometimes one or two aspects will become more evident. Besides love, perhaps I bear more joy than any other fruit. I wake up in the morning singing and go to bed at night still singing. There is always a song in my heart. Even when everything is going wrong, I still feel joy welling up inside of me, like a flame that can't be extinguished. Tears can be running down my cheeks, yet within me a song of praise is still being lifted up to God.

Problems don't end when you become a Christian. As you move out into ministry, you find that they may even increase, but the Lord gives the strength to bear them. Remember, the battle is not yours, but God's. How wonderful it is to take your burdens to Jesus and say, "Here are all my problems, Lord. I lift them up to You." He's the great Problem Solver.

It's not always easy to bring forth the fruit of the Spirit. Sometimes you have to become a fruit inspector and examine your own fruit. How much patience do you show when you're irritated by someone or something? What about the fruit of meekness? Sometimes meekness is thought of as weakness, but the word "meekness" actually means to be teachable and open to instruction. It can be very humbling to admit that you were wrong. when you were are so positive that you were right. Then there's the fruit of self-control? How well do you score on the anger test?

Fruit on a tree doesn't draw attention to itself, but rather brings honor to the owner of the orchard. As believers, our fruit should bring glory to our Father in heaven. Jesus said these words to His disciples when He walked on earth, *"My Father is glorified when you bear much fruit. The fruit is evidence that you are My disciples"* (John 15:8).

How wonderful it is to be a tree of righteous, a planting of the Lord, that He may be glorified.

CHAPTER 19

A FERVENT PRAYER
IS ANSWERED

Hallelujah! Aren't answered prayers wonderful? The Bible tells us that *"the effectual fervent prayer of a righteous man avails much"* (James 5:16). The salvation of Dwight was the result of fervent prayer, the prayer of a righteous woman named Martha who dared to believe that there is nothing too hard for God.

Dwight was what is called "a pillar" in the Presbyterian church. He had his hand in everything as an elder and the head of several church committees. He was strictly an intellectual with a Ph.D tacked at the end of his name, and he tended to think of himself as superior to everyone else. I was always uncomfortable around Dwight because of his high and mighty attitude and I avoided him as much as I possible. I used to sit in church, look at the back of his head and pray, "Father, help me to love this overbearing and unlovable man."

Sometime after we stopped attending the Presbyterian church, there was a congregational meeting to try to settle some of the differences that had arisen. Unfortunately, the church had become divided into two camps: believers and unbelievers.

This certainly isn't what God desires, but it has become the situation in many churches today.

In our former church, the believers desired that the church be fed a nourishing diet of Bible study, and the liberals were introducing sex education and guitar lessons into the Sunday School classes. Needless to say, Dwight was a liberal in the strongest sense of the word.

At the meeting, Dwight stood to his feet and declared, "If you people want to hear about the Bible, why don't you go down the road to the Orthodox Presbyterian Church where it's taught? Then everyone will have what they want and we can all be happy."

It was a strong statement for Dwight to make before the assembled congregation, and there was a moment of stunned silence. No one said a word in response. Finally the minister announced, "Let us close in prayer."

Martha's heart broke within her as she heard Dwight's words. She had loved and served the Lord for many years in the church, and she was filled with righteous indignation. Right there and then, she claimed Dwight for the kingdom of God and asked the Lord to save him.

That same night when Martha got home, she sat down at her desk and wrote Dwight a letter that went something like this:

"Dear Dwight, I was shocked at your statement at the meeting, but I want you to know that I still love you and that God loves you. I also want to let you know that I have placed your name at the top of my prayer list, and I intend to place your name on every prayer list that I can find. I am going to pray that God puts such a hunger for His Word into your heart that you will fall on your knees before Him in repentance, and come to know Jesus as your Lord and Savior. Remember that I will be praying for you every day until you become a believer. Lovingly, Martha."

Not only did Martha write the letter, but she mailed it to Dwight. There's that Holy Spirit boldness again. Martha had heard from God and was simply moving in obedience to His leading.

Martha prayed and prayed. For nearly a year she prayed for God to move upon Dwight's heart. I believe that hundreds more were also lifting him up daily before the throne of God. Martha had kept her promise to put Dwight's name on every prayer list in the area.

Then in late spring, Jack and I attended a large charismatic gathering and spotted Dwight sitting on the opposite side of the room.

Jack gave me a quick poke. "Look at that man over there in the fourth row. Who is that?"

"I know who it looks like, but it can't possibly be Dwight," I replied in utter and complete unbelief.

"It is Dwight!" Jack stated.

Miracles never cease. The person we were seeing was definitely Dwight, looking somewhat uncomfortable, but he was there nevertheless.

"I see it, but I just don't believe it," I told Jack.

We pray and then we are so amazed when God answers It shows how little faith we really have. The early disciples had the same trouble. In the Book of Acts chapter twelve, we read about Peter who had been arrested and put in jail. As you can imagine, all the Christians gathered and began to pray for his release. But when Peter was finally set free, and knocked on the door of the house where the other disciples were meeting in prayer, he was denied entrance. They refused to believe that it was actually Peter. "It's his angel," they decided. "It can't be Peter."

But Peter continued knocking, and when they finally opened the door and saw it was really him, we read that they were astonished! We often react the same way today when our prayers are answered.

Two months later, we once again saw Dwight at a meeting, and when the invitation was given to receive Jesus, he got out of his seat and went forward to open his heart to the Lord. Later that evening, I was asked to minister to a group of people who were seeking the baptism of the Spirit, and standing there among them was Dwight. I actually had the privilege of laying my hands upon him as he received the infilling of the precious Holy Spirit. With my own eyes, I witnessed the miracle of answered prayer. Dwight had become a Spirit-filled believer.

Dwight shared with us how it had all come about. Several months earlier a man had come to his office from Colorado on a temporary assignment and been given the adjoining desk. One evening, when the two of them were working late, they had gone out together to get something to eat. Over supper, the man had told Dwight an amazing story about how his wife had been healed of a long standing back ailment at a prayer meeting.

For the first time, Dwight heard about the Holy Spirit and learned that it is possible to have a personal relationship with the Living God. His heart was stirred and his interest aroused. When his new friend invited him to attend a meeting of the Full Gospel Business Men, Dwight saw first-hand the reality of the power of God and began to hunger to know the Lord.

Six weeks later, his assignment completed and his mission accomplished, the business associate returned to Colorado. The Lord had sent His messenger in answer to Martha's prayer that Dwight would hear the word and be saved. Dwight was transformed into a child of God.

Several months later, at the Presbyterian Church where Dwight had so violently waged his protest, he was granted permission to conduct a seminar on the Baptism of the Holy Spirit. He invited many Spirit-filled believers from local churches to attend. Dwight had been praying that God would reveal Himself to the congregation through the gifts of the Spirit with the evidence of signs and wonders.

"How is God going to bring us a message in tongues," Dwight asked, "if there is no one in the meeting who is willing and able to bring the message forth? I want everyone to be able to see the gifts of the Spirit in action."

There were probably sixty people assembled in the sanctuary the night of the seminar. Many were attending simply out of curiosity, wanting to learn about the change that had come into Dwight's life. Of course, Martha was there sitting on the front row, rejoicing in the spirit over answered prayer. Jack and I also made the decision to attend and hear what Dwight had to say. It was our first time back to our former church and it actually felt good to be in the old familiar setting again.

After opening in prayer, Dwight gave his testimony and answered some questions about the Holy Spirit. At the conclusion of his presentation, he prayed that the Lord would show forth His presence in our midst. Everyone waited expectantly for God to move. Finally, a young bearded man in the back of the church began to pray.

"Father, You have said that whatsoever we ask, we shall receive. So now, I ask in the name of Jesus, that You would speak to those gathered here in this place tonight. I pray that You will reveal Your Son to them in such a way that they will know beyond a shadow of a doubt that Jesus is alive and reigns today as King of kings and Lord of lords."

It was a simple prayer, wrapped in faith, and I knew that the Lord was going to answer his request. In the silence, everyone sat and waited. And then suddenly Jack began to speak in tongues. You could feel the power of God fill the sanctuary.

If anyone had ever told me two years before that Jack would be giving a message in tongues in this church, I would have laughed in unbelief. It only goes to prove that *"with God all things are possible"* (Luke 1:37).

127

Jack's message in tongues was quickly followed by the interpretation, and then the Lord continued to minister through several prophecies. It is hard to even describe the atmosphere in the place. Some began to weep and others dropped to their knees in prayer.

Suddenly the Spirit-filled believers scattered throughout the congregation began to sing in the spirit, their voices blending together in perfect harmony as the Heavenly Conductor led His choir in a hymn of praise. As the song ended, a hush fell upon the gathering and the unbelievers sat in awe experiencing the very presence of Almighty God in our midst. Several came forward to give their hearts to the Lord.

Not only had our prayers for a man been answered, but also our prayers for a church. What more can I say? Not only does God hear the prayers of His children, but He answers them. Jesus said, *"Hitherto have you asked nothing in My name: ask and you shall receive that your joy may be full"* (John 16:24).

That night my joy was full. I looked over at Dwight standing there praising the Lord in the church we had lifted up to the Lord so often, and my joy overflowed. My cup was running over as I joined with the congregation and sang, "How great Thou art! How great Thou art!"

CHAPTER 20
HELP MY UNBELIEF

When I started reading the Gospels, it seemed that nearly everywhere I looked, I saw something about demons. Intellectually I reasoned that demons were simply emotional problems and that Jesus called them demons so that the uneducated people to whom He ministered would understand in their simple minds. Certainly I didn't believe in demons. They sounded like something out of a Halloween story to me. As a Bible teacher, I avoided the subject if at all possible, and when forced into making a comment, I usually replied, "That's just an archaic word for mental and emotional illness." Let's be honest. I just plain didn't believe in demons. Maybe Jesus did, but I didn't.

"I believe everything in the Bible except for demons," I explained to the Lord, seeking to justify my position. There were even a few times when I considered tearing out a few pages to eliminate unexplainable portions.

Then one night I attended a Full Gospel Business Men's meeting where an anointed Spirit-filled Roman Catholic priest spoke. He shared about the love of Jesus and how the baptism of the Holy Spirit had changed his life and ministry.

At the close of the service a young man rushed forward flinging his arms around wildly and shouting, "You call yourself a Catholic priest, but you're not a priest. You're an agent of the devil." Curses rolled out of his mouth as he verbally abused the priest. Before anyone could react to his outburst, he began to strike out at the startled priest with his fists. Several men restrained him, and as he was being led away, he turned and looked directly at me. Through his eyes I saw something inhuman peering out, and I immediately knew that demons were real.

I was seeing someone who was definitely demonized and all my doubts were shed as I realized that *"we wrestle not against flesh and blood, but against principalities, against powers, against spiritual wickedness in high places"* (Ephesians 6:12). Satan had become a reality. Never again did I doubt that we are fighting an unseen spiritual enemy.

"Father," I prayed, "I just don't understand demons. What exactly is a demon?"

"My child, do you believe in germs?"

"Well, Lord, of course I do."

"Have you ever seen a germ?"

"No, not really."

"Yet germs are all around you and you are exposed to them all the time. Usually you are strong and healthy, so these germs don't cause you any difficulty. But if you become run down and are exposed to a germ, it can cause you to become ill. If left untreated, it can even cause death. Do you understand that?"

"Yes, Lord."

"Jean, a demon is a spiritual germ."

I finally understood. As long as I was spiritually healthy with the blood of Jesus coursing through my spiritual veins, I had nothing to worry about. But if I became spiritually weakened, a demon could attack and cause me to become spiritually ill and would even try to bring about my spiritual death.

"Thank You for that word of wisdom, Jesus."

How patiently the Lord teaches me, the same way you would teach a little child. I read many places in the Bible about being children of God, but nowhere about being adults of God. Certainly we are to become mature, but we are never to lose our childlike faith.

You can never expect to understand the Bible in one or two readings. Your understanding comes *"precept upon precept, precept upon precept, line upon line, line upon line, here a little and there a little"* (Isaiah 28:13). We begin reading the Bible as a preprimer and eventually it becomes a college textbook to us.

When I first started reading the Bible, I didn't understand anything. I was doing well if I could truly comprehend one verse per chapter.

"Lord, this is like reading Greek. What does all this mean?"

"Don't worry, little one. When you have read the Bible fifty times or so, all things will become clear."

Of course, with the Holy Spirit as my teacher, the Word of God has been opened to me. Each time I read the Word, more and more of it falls into place. In the Bible you have "See Dick run" in one verse and a scene from Hamlet contained in the next few verses. The simple and the complex are all mixed together. Every day that you study, you glean more and more of the wonderful truths of God that are available to those who search the pages of the holy scriptures. *"Study to show yourself approved unto God, a workman that does not need to be ashamed, rightly diving the word of truth"* (II Timothy 2:15).

With the knowledge that demons do exist stored away in the far corner of my mind, I walked happily down the path of the kingdom for a year. Then one day I felt compelled to buy a book on deliverance. I'm still not exactly sure why I bought it, as the subject of demons was one I tried hard to avoid, but God saw further down the path than I did.

As I perused the book, I could hardly believe what I was reading: demons speaking through people, throwing them onto the floor, coming out screaming. My heart believed what I was reading because it was scriptural, but my mind refused to grasp these things as fact.

"Lord, I believe. Help my unbelief," I prayed, quoting the words that I had read in Mark 9:24.

The very next morning there was a knock at the door and a woman from my Bible study stood there.

"I've got to talk to you," she said. "I have a real problem and I just don't know what to do about it."

I invited her to sit down and we chatted for a few minutes, making small talk until she could relax. Finally I said, "Tell me about your problem."

"I know I need deliverance," she blurted out.

I could hardly believe my ears. The Lord had sent someone to me who needed deliverance only one day after I had gone to Him in prayer about the subject. I had a feeling I was about to enter the school of the spirit for some instruction.

"I have a spirit of gluttony," she continued. "I don't want to eat so much. In fact, I hate myself for overeating, but I just can't control it. I have a picture of Jesus on the refrigerator door, but even that doesn't help. Yesterday I opened the fridge, took out two big handfuls of food, and then suddenly thought, What am I doing?"

By now tears were running down her face. "I went and flushed the food down the toilet, but five minutes later I was right back at the refrigerator, taking a whole package of cheese and cramming the slices into my mouth. What am I going to do? I can't go on like this."

Faith flooded my soul and I sensed the power of God come upon me. "We're going to pray right now and you are going to be set free."

So we prayed, thanking God for Jesus who had come to set the captive free. Then I spoke to the devil, reminding him that I had the authority to cast out demons in the name of Jesus. Taking a deep breath, I commanded, "You foul spirit of gluttony, you come out of this child of God right now!"

From her mouth came the loudest, most unearthly scream I have ever heard. The scripture ran through my mind, *"And they were all amazed and spoke among themselves saying, What a word is this! for with authority and power He commands the unclean spirits and they come out"* (Luke 4:36).

I had seen a demon come out first hand and I was amazed!

"Praise God!" the woman shouted. "I'm free from it! It's gone!"

Then suddenly her countenance changed. "I'm depressed," she stated in a shrill, wimpy little voice.

"You spirit of depression, you come out of her right now!"

And the demon did, followed by spirits of anxiety, nervousness, fear and self-pity. When she left my home an hour later, she was a new person, filled to overflowing with the Holy Spirit and aware that Jesus was not only her Savior, Baptizer and Healer, but also her Deliverer.

The Lord certainly answered my recent prayer when I had said, "I believe, help my unbelief." He had just given me a fast course in deliverance right by the book. I was able to declare positively, "I believe, I believe."

Well, that was just the beginning. The next evening about ten-thirty there was another knock at the door. This time Jack opened it to a young man named Michael. He had received the Lord at our Thursday night praise gathering several months before, but was still fighting drug addiction while struggling to walk in the ways of the Lord.

"I don't really know why I'm here," he told us. "I just didn't seem to be able to stay away. I truly had no intention of coming to your house tonight, but here I am in your living room."

Maybe Michael didn't know why he had come to see us, but I knew. The Lord wanted him be set free through the power of God.

We listened as Michel poured out his heart and described the frustration, anger and depression that held him in bondage.

No matter how hard he tried, he couldn't seem to overcome the addiction that plagued him.

"What you need is deliverance," Jack told him.

"Hey, man, that's crazy! I don't believe in Satan and little red demons running around with pitchforks and tails. You've got to be kidding."

We opened the Bible and read from the scriptures where Jesus had revealed Himself as Deliverer. Few people realize that one-fourth of Jesus' ministry was casting out demons.

Finally Jack said, "Look, what do you have to lose?"

"Nothing, I guess," Michael responded. "Okay, go ahead and cast these demons out of me. I need all the help I can get."

I'm not sure how much faith Michael had that night, but perhaps it didn't matter. The important thing was that Jack and I knew we had the power and authority over demons to cast them out. We had faith.

As we began to call forth the evil spirits, Michael started to sob and then to weep violently as in the power of God moved upon him. We were a part of a modern-day miracle as we witnessed a young man being set free. How long did it take? Twenty minutes? Thirty minutes? Time stood still as we experienced the presence of God in our midst.

All I know is that suddenly Michael announced, "It's over! The demons are gone! I'm free! I'm free at last! I know I'm free!"

So we began the ministry of deliverance to those in need. There is still so much we don't understand, but we continue to learn through trial and error and the leading of the Holy Spirit as the gift of discerning of spirits is manifested through us.

Our ministry is not advertized, but there is a steady stream of people who arrive at our front door seeking deliverance. This is not a popular ministry or one that the average servant of God seeks, but there is a sense of constant wonder and adoration as we see the captives set free from the prison of bondage.

One morning we got a phone call from the local Christian bookstore saying that they were sending us a troubled man who had some very serious emotional problems. It seems that he thought he had sold his soul to the devil.

We liked Alan, who was in his early twenties, immediately. He told us how he had come to know Jesus as a boy, but had turned away from Him while he was serving a tour in the army. Apparently, one night in a drunken rage, he had told the Lord that He didn't want Him living in his heart anymore and had entered into a pact with Satan. Just a few months later, Alan suffered a severe nervous breakdown and had been in and out of mental hospitals ever since, unable to live a normal life.

"I want to be a Christian and have Jesus come back into my heart again, but I gave my heart to Satan and now the mean old devil won't give it back," Alan informed us. Tears streamed down his face as he spoke. "My heart is the property of Satan and there is no hope for me."

Perhaps a psychiatrist would have written Alan off, but beneath all of the confusion and irrationality, we could sense a lost soul struggling to find his way back to the Father. Years of lies and torment had built a wall of unbelief that could only be broken through by the power of God.

Then the Lord gave us a word of knowledge that became the first step toward Alan's deliverance. It was just a baby step, but it was a step of faith nonetheless. "Perhaps you did give your heart to the devil, but don't you think that Jesus is strong enough to take it back? Don't you know that Jesus can bind up Satan and take possession of your heart again? Jesus certainly has much more power than the devil does."

We could see the truth settling upon Alan's understanding, and so his deliverance began. "Alan, listen carefully to the Word of God," Jack stated. *"He who the Son sets free, he shall be free indeed"* (John 8:26).

The moment of truth had come. "God wants you to be set free tonight. Jesus loves you and He has told me to command the devil to release your heart. It's going to happen right now," Jack declared with great authority. "In the mighty name of Jesus, I command Satan to loose your heart and return your heart to Jesus right now. We bind you, Satan, and Alan's heart is loosed from your grasp. Alan's heart is now the property of Jesus Christ!"

A smile began to break across Alan's face. "Yes, yes!" he stammered. "The devil doesn't have my heart anymore. Jesus has taken it back and He is living inside of me again. My heart belongs to Jesus."

Alan was heading in the right direction again. The truth had set him free. It was the beginning of a trip back to normalcy, but there was still a long way to go to total victory. I'm not going to pretend that the wall came tumbling down on Alan's first visit with us, but its destruction had definitely begun. The chains of bondage were falling away.

Alan became a frequent visitor at our home during the next two or three years, often sleeping in our guest room. We fed this precious child of God on love and the Word of God, building a foundation of Jesus Christ under him so that he could stand against the winds of fear and floods of despair that Satan continued to send upon him. We would often take Alan to church with us and hold his hands tightly because he would shake so violently as the battle raged within him under the preaching of the Word.

The deliverance of Alan was an ongoing thing, with a few demons being driven out at a time. The empty places they left were quickly filled with scriptures and fresh infillings of the Holy Spirit. Jesus had baptized Alan in the Spirit, granting him the power that was needed for him to survive as a Christian on the field of battle. Alan's favorite Bible verse became, *"Greater is He that is in me, than he that is in the world"* (I John 4:4). He knew that his victory was in Jesus and Jesus alone.

Then one Sunday evening, as we prayed together with Alan, an anointing of the Lord rested upon us and a prophecy came forth. *"On this night I will deliver you, My son, and you shall walk in peace all the days of your life."* The spirits that still remained came forth in a rush and it was all over. The Holy Spirit then fell upon Alan and filled him to overflowing. A young man, who was calm, peaceful and in his right mind, was standing before us with his hands lifted in praise to the Lord. The wall was gone.

With each passing day, Alan has continued to grow in strength, both spiritually and emotionally. As I write these words, he is has recently been hired by a local company to work in their warehouse and is planning to be married during the Christmas holidays. Alan is a walking miracle, a living witness to the power of God at work in the world today.

Not too long ago, the psychiatrist from the veteran's hospital called to ask what we had done to bring about the remarkable change in Alan. "Nothing," we replied. "It is the Lord who has made him whole."

We rejoice that the Lord still delivers his people from unclean spirits and that He truly is the same, yesterday, today and forever.

Yes, demons still exist today, but *"Greater is He that is in me than he that is in the world"* (I John 4:4). We have the victory. Jesus defeated Satan on the cross and we never need to fear him again. We have been given authority over evil spirits, and I praise God that He has given me the faith to use it. *"And these signs shall follow them that believe: In My name shall they cast out demons . . .* (Mark 16:1)

P.S. Alan has asked Jack to be his best man at the wedding.

CHAPTER 21

SOMEDAY, BUT NOT NOW

God never takes away our free will. We are not puppets, but free agents, free to choose whether we will follow Him or not. It's a big decision for most people and we need to weigh the cost of discipleship. Many step onto the scale and decide that the price is too great to pay, so they turn away from God's offer of salvation and continue down the broad path that leads to destruction.

I received a call from a friend asking me to talk with a woman who worked in his office. He was very concerned about Jane, who had been having physical problems and was scheduled for surgery in a few weeks. Her marriage had broken up and her young son had recently been diagnosed as borderline autistic.

"She has a tremendous need and seems to be open to the things of the Spirit," my friend informed me. "I think she would be very open to talk with you sometime this week."

A meeting was arranged for a few days later. When I stopped by to visit her, I found Jane to be a beautiful person with an obvious hunger to have the peace of God in her life. I shared my experience with her, explaining how Jesus had come to earth to die for our sins and that she could have eternal life through Him.

"After you receive Jesus as your Savior and become a child of God, you will find that your prayers are answered," I told her. "It's a wonderful thing to know that the Lord hears and answers your prayers."

"I know all about answered prayer," she informed me. "God answered a prayer of mine just a few months ago. I was very lonely and unhappy, so I prayed that the Lord would bring a nice man into my life who would love me. And God did. Just a week later, I met Dan."

"Praise the Lord!" I responded. "That's wonderful."

"There's just one thing though," she continued, "Dan's married. But he was lonely just like me and we're so good for each other. I know he'll never divorce his wife, but it doesn't matter. I just want to be with him. Some people might think that our relationship is wrong, but surely something so beautiful can't be a sin. I know that God has brought us together in answer to my prayer."

"Jane, your relationship is a sin," I stated bluntly. "Your relationship with this man is not of God. You're committing adultery and that is a sin."

Sometimes the word of God falls hard, and the messenger of the word is considered to be judgmental and harsh, but we must speak the truth as we are guided by the Spirit of Truth.

I had no choice but to tell Jane the truth. "If you want to come to Jesus, you must give up your relationship with this man. You must turn away from your sin. That's what the word "repentance" actually means."

Tears filled her eyes. "I just can't do it. I love Dan. If God is love, He surely doesn't mean for me to give up the man I love. That doesn't make any sense."

"But God is holy and He cannot condone your sin," I told her.

Silently she weighed the cost. "Then I don't want Jesus. Not if I have to give up Dan. I love Dan more than anything in the world and that's all that counts."

In the Bible there were great crowds that followed Jesus, and He spoke these words to them: *"Anyone who wants to be My follower must love Me far more than he does his own father, mother, wife, children, brothers or sisters. Yes, he must love Me even more than his own life, otherwise he cannot be My disciple"* (Luke 14:26). To that list, I'm sure that you can also add "married boyfriends" as well.

In essence, Jesus was just elaborating on the first and greatest commandment, *"You shall love the Lord your God with all your heart and with all your soul and with all your mind"* (Matthew 22:37). Jesus is saying that He must come first in our lives. He must be Number One.

As I stood up to leave, Jane put her arms around me. "Thank you for coming to tell me about Jesus. Maybe someday I'll receive Jesus as my Lord and Savior, but not now."

The Lord requires that we repent. That's not a very popular doctrine these days, but it's the doctrine that Jesus taught. Do you know the words of Jesus' first sermon after He came out of the wilderness? This is what it says in the Bible: *"From that time Jesus began to preach, saying, Repent for the kingdom of heaven is at hand"* (Matthew 4:17).

The Apostle Peter preached the same thing: *"Repent and be baptized every one of you in the name of Jesus Christ for the remission of sins and you shall receive the gift of the Holy Spirit"* (Acts 2:36). And the Apostle Paul also preached repentance saying, *"God now commands all men everywhere to repent"* (Acts 17:30). We must turn away from sin and strive for holiness. *"It is written, Be holy as I am holy"* (I Peter 1:16).

Jane's story is interesting in many ways because it shows how little people today know of God and what He expects from His followers. She is a product of the lukewarm teaching found in so many modern day churches. Let's look at some of the fallacies that Jane accepted as truths of God.

First, she was living under the misconception that God was hearing her prayers. Do you remember what she told me? These were her exact words: "I prayed that God would bring a nice man into my life who would love me. And He did."

However, the answer to her prayer was certainly not from God. The Lord would never have led Jane into an adulterous affair. The Bible clearly states that *"We know that God doesn't hear sinners, but if any man is a worshipper of God and does His will, God hears him"* (John 9:31). These are strong words.

We also read these words in the Bible: *"The eyes of the Lord are over the righteous and His ears are open to their prayers, but the face of the Lord is against those that do evil"* (I Peter 3:12). For over thirty years I prayed to God, not knowing that the only prayer He was going to hear from me was, "Lord have mercy on me, a sinner."

Secondly was this comment that Jane made: "Some people might think that what I'm doing is wrong, but surely something so beautiful can't be a sin." If Jane had read her Bible, she would have seen the verse in First John which states positively, *"Sin is the transgression of the law"* (I John 3:4). It also wouldn't take much searching of the scriptures to find these words of the law: *"You shall not commit adultery"* (Exodus 20:14). It isn't a question of whether Jane thinks her love affair is beautiful or not, but what God has to say about it in His Word.

The third misconception is in her statement, "If God is love, He surely doesn't mean for me to give up the man I love."

It's true that God is love, but if something is causing you to sin, then He certainly does mean for you to give it up. The Lord says, *"If your right hand offends you, cut if off and cast it away for you"* (Matthew 5:30). I love my children, but I certainly don't allow them to play with loaded guns. Warning them of imminent danger is a major demonstration of my love.

The fourth point in question is a rather common statement: "That doesn't make any sense." There's that old troublemaker

142

again, reason. That was Eve's problem in the garden of Eden. She had been given only one commandment: *"Don't eat from the tree of the knowledge of good and evil. You can eat of the other trees, but not that one"* (Genesis 2:16-17).

Then Satan came and tempted her. "That doesn't make any sense! It won't hurt you to eat from that tree too. Come on, God is love. Take a bite."

We want things to make sense. We always try to reason things out. We want to know why and why not. All kids are like that. They aren't willing to simply accept that "father knows best." They desire and even expect a logical explanation for everything that they are told to do.

God's children tend to have the same problem. Instead of recognizing the fact that "Father knows best" and accepting His decision, they murmur and complain and try to reason the whole thing out using their human intellect. The Word tells us, *"For My thoughts are not your thoughts, neither are your ways My ways, says the Lord. For as the heavens are higher than the earth, so are My ways higher than your ways and My thoughts than your thoughts"* (Isaiah 55:8-9).

It is God's desire that we trust Him completely. That's what faith is all about. God is love and if we simply walk in obedience, He will cause all things to work together for our good. We need to learn to follow the Lord's guidance without expecting any explanation on His part. It doesn't matter if we agree with His decision or understand the reasoning behind it. We are just called to walk in obedience, leaving the decisions in the capable hands of the Lord. We need to be obedient children who believe God with childlike faith. Whatever He says to you, do it.

Many times I make decisions for my children that they don't fully understand. They just have to accept the fact that in some matters I have far more wisdom and insight than they do and trust my guidance.

Our Heavenly Father ***always*** knows best. *"Trust in the Lord with all your heart and lean not to your own understanding"* (Proverbs 3:5).

Jane's <u>fifth</u> and the saddest statement of all was this, "Maybe someday I'll receive Jesus as my Lord and Savior, but not now."

As I left her apartment, I could only pray that "someday" comes before it's too late.

CHAPTER 22

THE WALLS ARE TUMBLING DOWN

God is doing a wonderful thing among His people. He is bringing them together, bone to bone, and uniting them in love. About three years ago, two women started coming to my house once a week so that we could read the scriptures together.

We decided to start reading in the Book of James and faithfully we would take turns reading the verses aloud. However, we had a big problem. We didn't understand what we were reading. I'm not saying that we weren't feeding our souls, but the word didn't seem to be penetrating our minds.

Finally we admitted that although it was wonderful to come together to study the Bible, we needed a teacher to instruct us in the meaning of the verses we were reading. Somehow, although I didn't know anymore about the scriptures than the other women, I was selected to become the teacher. I thought it was probably because we were meeting in my house, but looking back I know it was because the Lord was preparing me for my life's calling.

I wasn't even sure where to go to find a study book, but eventually I found my way to a bookstore located at a Baptist

Bible College about ten miles away. Finally after browsing through the books, I purchased a commentary on "The Epistle of James" by H. A. Ironside, an anointed biblical scholar who had been the pastor of Moody Bible Church in Chicago until his death in 1951. The Lord certainly directed me to choose this book from off the shelf, as such tremendous insight into God's Word was revealed through it to me. Dr. Ironside became my very first Bible teacher. Of course, the Holy Spirit is my Heavenly Teacher. The Spirit *"has been given to teach believers all things"* (John 14:26), so without His presence, I could never have understood anything from the Bible, much less taught it. But Dr. Ironside's books were such a blessing to me as I sought wisdom and understanding of the Word of God.

So our little group forged forward. I would study to keep one chapter ahead of my students and then share my newfound knowledge with them when we met. With only five chapters in James, it didn't take us long to finish our study, so we decided to look together into the Gospel of John. I made another trip to the bookstore to purchase another book by Dr. Ironside.

Meanwhile, the Lord continued to add to our small group, and almost before we knew it, we were numbering over twenty women that were gathering together every Wednesday. At first we were partakers of the good milk of the Word, but as time passed and we increased in our understanding, the diet was changed to stronger meat. The babes in Christ were rapidly growing in the Lord and becoming spiritually mature.

During the past two years over a hundred women have walked through our front door to be fed upon the word of God. I've lost count of how many have actually received the Lord and been baptized in the Holy Spirit on Wednesday mornings. As we continue to gather together unto Him every week, our hearts flow as one and there exists a bond between us that is hard to describe.

One morning we counted the denominations that were represented in the group and found that we came from twelve different denominations. The walls of division have tumbled down in the kingdom of God and we can join together as one in the name of Jesus. The name of Jesus is the only name that saves us. It is not being called Presbyterian, Roman Catholic, Lutheran, Methodist or Baptist that saves us, but only the wonderful name of Jesus Christ.

Occasionally someone will ask me what church one of the women in the group attends. I will just smile as I tell them that I'm not really sure where any of the women go to church. When we come together on Wednesday mornings, the only name that really matters is the name of Jesus.

I once heard a story about a duck pond that was a gathering place for many ducks. The ducks all looked pretty much alike, but the pond was divided by concrete barriers that kept the ducks from mixing together. Each group of ducks swam around in their own partitioned area, enjoying fellowship only with those who were in their particular flock.

One group of little ducks was swimming around and they kept dunking one another under the water. Obviously these were the Baptist ducks. Then in another partition were ducks who constantly were crossing themselves. Yes, they were the Catholic ducks. And of course there were the Methodist ducks who were paddling around methodically in little squares. The Presbyterian ducks were sprinkling each other with water in their section, while the Episcopalian ducks were swimming around with waterproof prayer books tucked under their wings in another area. And we don't want to forget the Pentecostal ducks who were quacking in tongues.

These little ducks never had any contact with each other. They were totally separated by the concrete barriers and it looked like they would never come together.

Then suddenly the rain began to fall, and it rained and rained and rained. The rain came down in torrents day after day. The water in the duck pond rapidly began to rise higher and higher, and soon it was flowing over the barriers that had divided the little ducks from one another for so very long.

It was like a mighty flood, and almost before the ducks had time to realize what was happening, they were all were swimming around in the pond together. And do you know what? As the ducks came together, they were all quacking in tongues and you couldn't tell one from the other.

That's a pretty good description of what is happening in the current move of God. The Lord is pouring out His Spirit upon all flesh as the latter rain flows down from heaven. God's people have been separated by so many walls of doctrine and tradition, but now the Holy Spirit is drawing us together and making us one.

The Lord really only has one church. We may attend different churches, but there is only one church. The church is not a building, but rather the church is made up of all those who are building a new life in Christ Jesus. The individual churches we attend are really only small families in the community of God.

In the Gospel of John, the Lord Jesus prayed a powerful prayer for His disciples. *"May they all be one, as You Father are in Me and I am in You, that they also may be one in us so that the world may believe that You have sent Me* (John 17:21).

Many times at the close of a meeting, we will all join hands and sing this simple chorus together: "Father, make us one. Father make us one, that the world may know Thou hast sent Thy Son, Father make us one."

The Lord commands that we love one another. *"A new commandment I give unto you, that you love one another as I have loved you, that you also love one another. By this shall all men know that you are My disciples, if you have love one for another"* (John 13:34-35).

The walls of division have been broken down. The dry bones are coming together and receiving new life. The body of Christ is being united as the Holy Spirit is poured out upon us. Let us rejoice and be glad.

Loving one another is not an option. It is a commandment. Beloved, let us love one another.

CHAPTER 23

THE PRODIGALS

Several weeks ago a woman called on the phone and asked us to come by and talk with her husband who had become very depressed and unhappy. "Phil just mopes around the house all the time and I'm at my wits' end," she told us. "I hate seeing him so miserable, but I just don't know what to do. I know that the only solution is Jesus and I have a feeling that Phil would listen to you."

His wife wasn't exaggerating. We found Phil to be a very melancholy person. He slumped down on the sofa and informed us, "Life is such a drag. I sometimes wonder if it's worth the effort. I wake up in the morning and force myself to get out of bed. I love my wife and kids, but there's this terrible emptiness inside of me."

"That emptiness you're experiencing is caused by a spirit-shaped void," Jack informed him, "and only Jesus can fill it. Man was created spirit, soul and body, but because of sin, your spirit is dead. Jesus is the Way, the Truth and the Life, and He wants to come in and bring life to your spirit. Jesus will make you into a whole man, filling that empty spot within you."

"I know I need something because I can't go on like this," Phil said. "Not only am I miserable, but I'm making my entire family the same way. I don't know about Jesus though. When I was about twelve years old, I went to vacation Bible school and asked Jesus to come into my heart. For three days, I felt wonderful."

Phil paused for a few moments as though he was reflecting back in time. "I can still remember the feeling I had then. It was like I was clean all over. But the feeling didn't last, and I guess I just sort of forgot all about Jesus. If I ever had a chance to get right with God, I sure blew it back then." Phil sighed and lit another cigarette.

Another backslider! We have found the world to be full of backsliders, those who once knew Jesus but have turned away from Him for one reason or another. They are like little seeds that were planted in the soil and began to grow, but then failed to survive because of shallow root systems and thorns that choked them out.

Jesus told a parable about seeds falling on rocky soil where there was little depth of earth. The plants sprang up quickly enough in the shallow soil, but the hot sun soon scorched them and they withered and died because they had so little root. Other seeds fell among the thistles and the thistles choked out the tender blades.

The Living Bible explains it this way: *"The shallow rocky soil represents the heart of a man who hears the message and receives it with real joy, but he doesn't have much depth in his life and the seeds don't root very deeply. After a while, when trouble comes, or persecution begins because of his beliefs, his enthusiasm fades and he drops out. The ground covered with thistles represents a man who hears the message, but the cares of this life and his longing for money choke out God's Word and he does less and less for God"* (Matthew 13:20-22).

There are many backsliders and many reasons for their present condition. We might be looking at a little boy who loved Jesus, but was teased by his friends for carrying his Bible to school, so he hid it away in his dresser drawer and never read it again. Or perhaps the backslider is a pretty seventeen-year-old girl who didn't want to be branded as a "Jesus freak," so she turned away from the Lord and back to the world. Or what about the family man who was too busy earning a living to read his Bible or go to church? These are just a few examples of seedlings who perished before they really put down roots or bore any fruit.

Phil was one of them. His childhood experience with Jesus had faded into a fuzzy memory, so he had turned his back on the kingdom of God and gone his own way. Jesus told us that there are two roads. There is a broad road that leads to destruction and a narrow road that leads to life. You are on one or the other.

Phil was on the broad road and had been traveling it for many years. But now Jesus was calling to him saying, *"Follow Me!"* Phil had come to a crossroads in his life. He was being given the opportunity to move from the broad road to the narrow. He had entered into the valley of decision.

But God had not forgotten Phil, and as he shared with us about the lonely years and the hardships he had endured, it was easy to see God's hand had been upon him every step of the way. We could sense the presence of God filling the room.

"Do you remember the story of the prodigal son?" I asked.

"No, I don't think so. I never have read the Bible very much."

We Christians take it for granted that everyone knows certain Bible stories: the loaves and the fishes, the good Samaritan, Peter walking on the water, and Jesus as the Good Shepherd.

But it is amazing that people who have warmed church pews all of their lives know so little about the Bible. The unchurched know even less. Most people know about Adam and Eve, Noah and the ark, and thanks to the movie, "The Ten Commandments," they know about Moses. In the New Testament they are familiar with the Christmas story and the resurrection of Jesus, but little else. I mourn over the ignorance in the world today about God's Word. Yet I understand, for I once walked in the same darkness.

I leaned forward on my chair and began to share the story of the prodigal son from Luke chapter fifteen with Phil. "Once there was a man who had two sons, and one day the younger son asked his father for his share of the inheritance. When he received the money, he left home and went far away where he spent all of his inheritance on wine, women and song until he had nothing left. A famine came upon the land and things got worse and worse for the young man. Finally he reached the bottom of the pit, feeding pigs in a foreign land."

As I spoke, the anointing of the Holy Spirit came upon me and the words of this simple story were quickened, made alive.

"There the prodigal son sat in the muck and mire of the pigpen, remembering how wonderful it had been when he had lived at home in his father's house. Right there and then, he made the decision to return to his father and admit how wrong he had been. He stood to his feet and leaving the pigpen behind, he headed down the road toward home. He still had a good way to go, when he saw his father running toward him with his arms outstretched, so happy to see him coming back home."

I paused and then continued, "Phil, you're that son and God loves you so very much. He wants you to come home."

"Oh God, I'm so sorry," Phil sobbed. "Father, take me back. I want to come home and be with You."

Jack dropped to his knees beside Phil and led him in a simple prayer of repentance. A twentieth century prodigal had returned.

Mark was another prodigal. A youth leader in the local Catholic church, loaded with potential as a worker in God's kingdom, Mark was our "golden boy." We clucked over him as proud spiritual parents, thanking God for entrusting us with this precious soul. We fed him on the Word and spent hours pouring our lives in him.

But, a struggle was going on inside of Mark that we weren't aware was taking place. The world was calling to him, tempting him to leave the things of God and go back to his old ways. When we receive Jesus as Lord, we need to remember that though we are still *in* the world, we are not *of* the world. Mark was in the middle of a spiritual tug-of-war for his soul.

Mark attended the senior prom with a really nice Christian girl, so the next day when he showed up at our house, we expected to hear all about the events of the prior evening. Were we ever in for a surprise.

"I've come to turn in my Bible," Mark informed us sarcastically. "I'm tired of being a Christian, tired of being good, tired of having people make fun of me. I've had it. The prom was absolutely horrible. Everyone was drinking, and there I sat holding a Coke. Everyone was making out with their girlfriends, and there I was holding hands with a "sister." I don't want to be good anymore." And then he turned and walked away, leaving us standing there in utter amazement at what we had just heard.

We only saw Mark one time during the entire summer that followed. At two-thirty one morning, he pounded on our front door, so drunk he could hardly stand up. Jack pulled a pair of pants on over his pajamas and spent over an hour sitting on the porch with Mark, ministering love to a boy who was being torn apart inside. But Jack's words seemed to fall on deaf ears.

There wasn't a day that passed that summer when we didn't lift Mark up to the Lord in prayer. We phoned him a few times and left a message, but our calls were never returned. Mark completely ignored us. He had not only turned his back on God, but also on us. All we could do was continue to believe that the Lord would draw him back into the fold.

Then in early fall, Mark called on the phone. "I've got to see you right now," he said. "You've probably heard that I'm going to be attending college in London. Actually, I'm leaving for Europe tomorrow. I can't go overseas without Jesus in my heart. My life is so empty without the Lord. Please, can I come over so you can pray with me to get right with God?"

Another prodigal returning, and God's arms outstretched to receive him home. When you have eaten of the heavenly food, the things of earth are dull and tasteless.

It only took a simple prayer and Mark was forgiven and restored. *"If we confess our sins, He is faithful and just to forgive us our sins and to cleanse us from all unrighteousness"* (I John 1:9). So with our blessing, we sent off our first overseas' missionary.

God loves us so much. Jesus hung upon the cross at Calvary and with His own blood, He wrote this message for all mankind: *"I LOVE YOU!"*

It is through Jesus that we experience the love that passes all understanding. He is the Shepherd who seeks the lost sheep and then says, *"Rejoice with Me for I have found My sheep which was lost"* (Luke 15:6).

The Father is still calling to the prodigals, *"Come home!"*

CHAPTER 24

RALPH

Jack sat on the floor with the boys and finished telling them the message of the Gospel. "That's all there is to it. Don't you want to ask Jesus into your heart right now as your Lord and Savior?"

They glanced around at each other, checking out reactions. Finally the oldest boy spoke up. "Let me think about it for a while. It's a serious step and I don't want to rush into anything." The others two boys shook their heads in agreement with his statement.

Their mother had recently started attending my Bible study and she had invited us over to talk to her children about the Lord. She was the mother of three really nice young men. Andy was thirteen, David was fifteen and Ralph was nearly seventeen. As Jack spoke, they had listened attentively to every word that he said. The presence of God had been obvious, but apparently it was a time of seed sowing and not of reaping.

In the car on the way home, Jack remarked, "If only they hadn't been all together, I'm sure they would have received Christ. Had I just been able to talk to each of the boys separately, I'm certain the result would have been different. Or if just one of them had responded positively, they probably would have all said yes. None of them wanted to be the one to make the decision. Boys are like that."

"It just wasn't the right time," I replied. "God knew what was going to happen. At least now they know the truth."

A week later Ralph came with his parents to a Saturday night meeting that was being held at a local school. Jack and I had taken a step of faith, and along with some other believers, rented the building to show the movie, "Gospel Road," a Christian film starring Johnny Cash. We were pleasantly surprised to see that over two hundred people had made the effort to attend.

The movie, a dramatic enactment of the life of Christ, was very touching and we saw several in the audience wiping their eyes as it ended. At the close of the meeting, one of the local pastors went forward and gave an invitation to receive Jesus. Not one hand was raised in response.

Again the invitation was given. "If God has been speaking to your heart tonight, raise your hand and someone will pray with you to receive Jesus." But still no hand was lifted.

Led by the Spirit, Jack suddenly walked to the back of the auditorium and stopped beside where Ralph was seated. "Hasn't God been speaking to you tonight, Ralph?" Jack asked him.

"Yes, I guess that He has."

"Are you ready to ask forgiveness for your sins and receive Jesus as your Lord and Savior?"

Ralph made his decision. "Yes, I am."

Jack and Ralph left the room and went out into the back hall. There Ralph prayed and gave his heart to the Lord. The greatest of all miracles took place and Ralph was born again as a child of God. I know that the angels in heaven were rejoicing along with us.

Jack had some final instructions for Ralph. "I want you to go back in there and tell someone what Jesus has done for you tonight."

As we watched, Ralph returned to the auditorium and stepped up to a group of young people and told them he had just prayed and received Jesus as his Savior. It's so important that we are not ashamed of Jesus, but that we openly acknowledge that He is our Lord and Savior. There should be no closet Christians.

"For with the heart man believes unto righteousness and with the mouth confession is made unto salvation. For the scripture says, Whosoever believes on Him shall not be ashamed" (Romans 10:10-11).

Three weeks later I was teaching one of my Bible study groups when there was a knock at the door. It was Ralph's father. He entered the room and quickly went to where his wife was seated.

"Wilma, there's been an accident and they're taking Ralph to the hospital. I've just been contacted and they want us to come right over."

"What happened?" Wilma asked him. "How bad is it?"

"They didn't say. All they told me is that Ralph has been in an automobile accident and he was being taken to the hospital. That's all I know."

"Oh, God," Wilma exclaimed as she put on her coat, "please don't let it be anything serious."

"Let's pray before you leave to go see him," I insisted. Everyone in the room bowed their heads and we went to the One who is all knowing. "Father, we just entrust Ralph into Your loving care. Place Your healing hand upon him and be with him. Give comfort to this family and fill them with Your peace right now. Thank You, Jesus."

There was only time for that short prayer before Wilma and her husband left for the hospital. We all sat there stunned, trying to take in what had just happened. It's amazing how quickly a storm can come up. One minute the sun is shining, and the next minute the dark clouds come rolling in. We could only wait and pray.

I remembered that the family had no church home. Wilma had only been saved for a short time and had just started coming to my Bible class about a month before. I knew that I needed to call Jack at work and make him aware of what had happened. "Ralph's been in an accident and no one knows how bad it is," I told him. "Why don't you call the emergency room and see if you can learn something about his condition? Everyone from the Bible study is still here at the house and we're praying together."

In a few minutes, Jack called back. "There were two boys involved in the accident and one of them didn't make it. I couldn't find out if Ralph is dead or alive. I'm leaving work right now to go to the hospital."

The living room was filled with the sounds of the women praying in the spirit. We really didn't know how to pray. *"For we don't even know what we should pray for, nor how to pray as we should: but the Holy Spirit prays for us with such feeling that it cannot be expressed in words. And the Father who knows all hearts knows, of course, what the Spirit is saying as He pleads for us in harmony with God's own will"* (Romans 8:26-27 TLB).

Then the phone rang again. This time it was Wilma. "He's dead, Jean. Ralph is dead. Can you come to the hospital to be with me?"

Our minds cry out, "Why, God? Why did this happen?"

But that still small voice within speaks to our heart with the familiar words, *"All things work together for good to those that love God, to those who are the called according to His purpose"* (Romans 8:28).

Even as I drove along the Parkway to the hospital, the Lord was speaking to my heart and saying, *"He is not dead, but he lives."* I knew that Ralph had died physically, but I also knew that he had everlasting life and would never perish.

The story comes to mind about a man who had beautiful roses growing in his garden. One day he decided to go out and pick one to bring into his house. He looked at all of the roses, seeking the perfect one to bring inside. Then he spotted a rosebud that had just begun to open. "That's the one," he thought, and stooping down, he cut it and carefully carried it into his house.

That was Ralph, a bud just starting to open, just entering manhood. He was a perfect rose, without spot or blemish. All of his sins had been washed away in the blood of Jesus and he was safely in the hand of the Heavenly Gardener. God had made a decision and taken Ralph home. We do not have the right to question why. *"Doesn't the potter have power over the clay...?"* (Romans 9:21). He is the Potter and we are the clay. In faith, we must trust the Lord in every situation.

I arrived at the hospital, entered the family room and wrapped my arms around Wilma, holding her tightly as she wept. "Oh, Lord," I prayed within, "there is nothing that I can say. All I can do is let her know that I love her."

And within came His response, *"Don't you know that love is the greatest gift that you can possibly give?"*

Death is never pleasant and it is recorded in the Bible that when Lazarus died, Jesus wept (John 11:35). We need to learn not only to *"rejoice with those that rejoice, but to weep with them that weep"* (Romans 12:15). What comfort there was in the fact that Ralph had received Jesus. Our concern was not for Ralph because we knew where he was. Rather, our concern was for the loved ones that he left behind.

Amid the tears and heartbreak, the Lord was moving upon hearts. Just a few hours after Ralph died, while we were still at the hospital, his girlfriend asked Jesus to come into her heart. And later that evening, his two brothers expressed their belief in the Lord Jesus Christ as Savior. As a result of Ralph's death, others were experiencing spiritual life.

What comfort can be found in the words of Jesus: *"I am the resurrection and the life. He that believes in Me, even though he is dead, yet shall he live: and whosoever lives and believes in Me, shall never die"* (John 11:25-26).

Ralph's high school friends flocked to the funeral home and stood by the open coffin, face to face with eternity. Jack and I were able to share with them about Jesus and the eternal life that is offered to those who believe. Young people who would never set foot in a church, attend a Billy Graham meeting or read a Bible were listening attentively to the gospel message.

On Monday morning, Jack conducted the funeral service for Ralph. He related how only three weeks before, Ralph had opened his heart and received salvation and eternal life. "Ralph had the presence of mind to grab hold of a good thing when he was given the opportunity. It is my prayer that all of you will have the same presence of mind. Today can be your day of salvation. Don't leave this place without asking Jesus into your heart."

We buried Ralph on a bleak cloudy day in February. I looked at his mother's face as we stood by the grave and I saw the heartbreak of death. Yet as I looked upon her face, I also saw the heart of God revealed through her. I had a greater understanding of how God must have felt when He looked down from heaven and saw His Son hanging on the cross, giving His life that we might have life.

Suddenly the clouds parted and the sun came shining through, casting a golden glow over the cemetery. At that moment, I knew without a doubt that God is always there, even when He doesn't appear to be. Sometimes clouds may hide the sun from our view, but the sun is always still there. And sometimes problems will hide God from our view, but He is still there, loving us and working out His perfect plan in our lives.

"There is a time to be born and a time to die" (Ecclesiastes 3:2). It was Ralph's time to die and God had reached out three weeks earlier and revealed to Ralph the key that would open the door of eternity. What is the key? The key is to put your faith in Jesus as your Savior and Lord.

Sixteen years doesn't seem like a very long time to spend on earth, yet it was how much time God allotted to Ralph. Jesus was here on earth for a brief thirty-three years, and His actual ministry only lasted for three and a half years. In our natural minds, it is easy to think that Jesus could have accomplished much more if He had lived for an additional forty years. Yet as He hung on the cross, Jesus cried out in a loud voice, *"It is finished!"* (John 19:30). His work on earth was complete. There was nothing more that remained for Him to do. Jesus had accomplished the Father's will.

Somehow I feel that God spoke to Ralph and said, *"Come on, son. Your time on earth is finished."* Then He just reached down from heaven and took Ralph home.

CHAPTER 25
LIFE OUT OF DEATH

God often uses death to draw little lost sheep into the fold. God's ways are not our ways and He certainly proved it during the following incident that involved my neighbor from across the street.

Joan is much more than a neighbor to me. She is one of my very best friends. When she was only eighteen, Joan was diagnosed with multiple sclerosis, a progressive muscle disease which has crippled her body and kept her confined to a wheelchair for over fifteen years. When I first met Joan, she had already lost the use of her legs, but she was still able to use her hands. Then as the years passed, even her hands ceased to function. Joan could no longer feed herself or even hold a book. Her speech became difficult to understand.

Fortunately Joan had a devoted husband and a competent housekeeper, who provided constant care for her. She was a naturally optimistic person with a sunny disposition, who always seemed to rise above her physical problems.

You can imagine that the desire of my heart was to see Joan completely healed and to live a normal life. I will never forget the morning that I was kneeling by the bed making intercession for her.

"Lord, I would give anything to see Joan healed?"

"Do you really mean that, Jean?"

"Yes, Lord. I love her so much that I would do anything."

"Do you love her enough to exchange places with Joan so that she can be free to live a normal life?"

I had to really think about that question. I certainly loved Joan, but how could I possibly agree to get into her wheelchair and take on her affliction. I loved her, but I had to admit that I didn't love her that much. I had no choice but to tell the Lord that my love for Joan didn't qualify as sacrificial love.

"I love her, Lord, but not nearly enough to take her place."

"My Son loved you so much that He took your place on the cross so that you could be free."

I was humbled before my God as I saw how great His love was for me, and I also realized just how far I had to go before I could show forth the God- kind of love to others.

So Joan remained in her wheelchair and I continued to love her to the best of my ability. One of my major goals in life was to introduce Joan to the Lord. I wanted Joan to invite Jesus into her heart and be born again.

Looking back, I think that Joan was probably one of the first people that I witnessed to about my divine encounter with Jesus. She was my little congregation of one and was truly a captive audience. There was no way Joan could escape my preaching. She heard about Jesus every day when I stopped by her house for my usual visit.

But there was a wall of doubt surrounding Joan. Some people have a hard time believing that Jesus will actually take away their sins and come and live within them. Joan was numbered among the doubters. She wanted to believe, but she just couldn't get past her unbelief.

I don't know how many times Joan asked Jesus to come into her heart. She would wait impatiently for a few minutes, and then turn and ask me, "Do you think that He came in?"

"Of course, He did," I would assure her. "You asked Jesus in and He is now living in your heart. Your sins have all been forgiven."

However, the next day when I would stop by to see Joan, she would once again be overcome with doubt. "How do I know that Jesus really came into my heart? I don't feel any different today."

As humans, we rely so much on our feelings, when we should be relying upon the Word of God. *"Lo I stand at the door and knock. If any man hears My voice and opens the door, I will come in to him" (Revelation 3:20).* Those are the exact words of Jesus quoted directly from the Bible.

It's important for new Christians to understand that they're probably not going to feel any different at first. It's a lot like getting married. Two people stand before a minister and hear the words, "I now pronounce you man and wife." Do they immediately look any different? Of course not. And probably they don't even feel very married at first. But they are. Why? Because a man of authority has pronounced them married, and the two are now viewed as one.

In the same way, we come before God and make our vow to spend the rest of our lives with Him. The Lord proclaims, *"You are now My child. Your sins are forgiven. You have become a Christian."*

It doesn't matter if you don't feel different. Just believe that God's words have changed you and given you new life in Christ. Then as you walk hand in hand with Him, your belief will become a reality. *"As many as received Him to them God gave power to become the sons of God, even to those that believe on His name"* (John 1:12). The Bible says it and all you have to do is believe it.

As the weeks and months passed, I still could not convince Joan that Jesus had truly saved her and made her a child of God. She knew it in her mind, but she just didn't seem to be able to get that knowledge down in her heart. Jack calls the distance from head to heart, the longest fourteen inches in the world."

But God was about to reveal Himself to Joan in a very dramatic set of circumstances that would forever change her life. Late one night her husband received a phone call informing him that his father had died of a heart attack in Pennsylvania. It wasn't easy for Joan to travel, but there was no choice. The next day they made the six hour drive and when Joan arrived, she was completely exhausted. The family was going to meet at the funeral home at four o'clock and afterwards go to a cousin's house for an old-fashioned Irish wake.

"I'm so tired right now that I'd really rather just stay here at the house and rest. Do you think that could be worked out somehow?" Joan asked.

So arrangements were quickly made for a neighbor to come and stay with Joan during the family's absence. The woman would be available to answer the phone, change channels on the television or go to the door if necessary since Joan was unable to do any of those things for herself.

"You'll probably be more comfortable on the couch," Joan's husband remarked as he lifted her out of the wheelchair. "You might as well relax while we're gone. It will probably be four or five hours before we return, but Florence will be here if you need anything." Giving Joan a quick kiss on the cheek, Joe was gone.

After spending a few minutes getting acquainted, the two women settled down on the couch to watch television together. About a half an hour later Florence said, "I have a terrible headache. I think I'll go see if I can find some aspirin in the medicine cabinet to take."

In just a few moments, she returned to the living room and sat back down on the sofa next to Joan. "I couldn't find any, but the headache will pass. It's no problem." They continued watching the television program.

Suddenly, Florence made a low moan and slipped down on the couch. "What is it? Are you all right?" Joan asked. There was no response. Nothing. Florence's eyes were wide open, but unseeing. She was lying there completely still, and Joan knew without a doubt that the woman was dead there beside her on the couch.

Joan was almost overcome with panic. Alone and unable to move, she cried out to the Lord, "God, help me!"

Then audibly, she heard the voice of God. *"Don't be afraid. You are not alone. Lo, I am with you always, even unto the end of the world."*

It was a gentle voice, the still small voice of the Savior. A peace flooded Joan's soul and she knew that Jesus was living in her heart. She was not facing this ordeal alone, and she knew that she would never be alone again. God was with her and within her.

"All right, Jesus," Joan responded. "You know that there is absolutely nothing that I can do about this. I'm going to have to trust You completely. I know that You answer prayer, so I'm going to ask You to send my husband home to me right now. He's not supposed to come home for at least another four hours, but I need him now."

Joan glanced down at Florence and then quickly looked away. "I'm not going to look at this poor woman who's lying here beside me. Instead I'm going to keep my eyes upon You. Please help me keep my mind on You instead of allowing my fear to overcome me."

Joan's husband was still at the funeral home when he felt an immediate urgency to be with Joan. It was like nothing that Joe had ever experienced before in his life.

"You all go ahead to the dinner," he told his family. "I need to stop by the house and check that Joan is all right. I think that something's wrong."

"Don't be ridiculous," his aunt replied. "Florence is with her and everything's fine. It's out of our way to stop by the house." "I don't care. I need to be with Joan."

Fifteen minutes later, Joe arrived at the house. Walking into the living room, he noticed Florence lying next to Joan on the couch. "Has she fallen asleep?" he asked somewhat concerned.

"No, Florence is dead. She's died about thirty minutes ago. But I haven't been here alone. Jesus has been here with me tonight, and I know that He'll be with me always. God is so good."

In a time of death, Joan received new life. She had been born again.

I no longer try to second guess God. His ways are so much higher than mine. As a little child, I just accept in faith what my Father is doing in my life and the lives of those around me.

Today Joan has the assurance of her salvation and is a beautiful Spirit-filled Christian. She has a bumper sticker across the back of her wheelchair that states positively, "Happiness is knowing Jesus." Joan has been healed spiritually. That's miracle number one. Now we are believing for her physical healing and miracle number two. With God all things are possible.

CHAPTER 26

YESTERDAY

Walking with the Lord is always so exciting and wonderful. You never know what's going to happen. That's why every day is a great adventure. Let me tell you what took place in my life yesterday.

I need to start by telling you that several days before, a woman who regularly attends my Bible study had called to tell me that she would be missing class that morning. Beth had phoned to explain that her mother, who was visiting from Arkansas, had recently fallen and broken two of her ribs, so there was no way she could be left alone.

I certainly understood her situation and appreciated that she had taken the time to phone me. However, as far as I was concerned, it was just one of those little pieces of information that you file away in a far corner of your mind and never think of again.

Yesterday, as I was doing the ironing, the Lord spoke clearly to me. *"I want you to take a bottle of oil and drive over to Beth's house. You are to pray for her mother and anoint her with the oil."*

Sometimes when God speaks it is with such authority, you don't even hesitate a minute before obeying. I quickly unplugged the iron, grabbed the oil and my purse, and headed out to the car. I had never been to Beth's house before, but I drove there without any difficulty. Obviously the Lord was leading and guiding me through the streets of my town to her home.

I was surprised when a man opened the door, since I fully expected to find Beth standing there. "You must be Beth's husband," I said. "I don't think we've ever met before."

"No, I'm just a friend," he replied. "Since I'm not working right now, Beth asked if I would come and stay with her mother while she went to the store. Did you want to see Beth?"

"Not really. I just dropped by to see how her mother was doing today," I explained. "I can come back later."

"It's no problem at all. Mrs. Daniel is right here in the living room," the man replied. "Come on in. She'll be glad to have some company."

I found Beth's mother sitting in the big recliner by the fireplace, obviously in a great deal of pain. She was probably in her middle seventies and lines of suffering were etched on her face.

After a few minutes of getting acquainted, I announced, "I've come to anoint you with oil and pray for your recovery. Do you mind if I read you some scripture from the Bible?"

I'm not really sure if she answered me or not. Anyway, I just opened my Bible and started reading from the sixth chapter of Mark about how the disciples went out *"and anointed with oil many that were sick and healed them."* Then I gently put my hand upon her and prayed a simple prayer. I had confidence that I was on a divine assignment and that everything was moving according to God's plan.

When I finished praying, Beth's friend introduced himself. "I should have told you my name sooner. I'm Tom Dudley. What church are you representing?"

"Actually, I'm not representing any church. I'm just a Christian who loves Jesus." I then shared with the two of them how I had met Jesus three years before and the way He had changed my life. "I really didn't know it was possible to be filled with so much joy and peace," I added

"I know exactly what you mean," Tom responded. "Jesus also came into my heart recently and forgave all my sins. And you're certainly right, the joy and peace that is experienced is amazing."

Suddenly Mrs. Daniels spoke up, "How I wish that Jesus would come into my heart so I could have that joy and peace in my life too."

Her comment almost took my breath away. God works in ways that absolutely astound me. It appeared that my mission hadn't been completed. There was still work to be done, and I had nearly missed the opportunity.

Turning my full attention to Beth's mother, I asked, "Do you want to pray right now and receive Jesus as your Savior?"

"That would be wonderful," she said with a little smile.

I knelt down beside her and led her in the sinner's prayer. Of course, I didn't actually see Jesus enter her heart, but as I looked at her tear-stained face, I saw the worry lines smooth away and a peace settle upon her.

Sensing the moving of God is very much like observing the wind. You can't see the wind, but you know it is there because you notice the leaves move on the trees and the grass ripple as the wind blows across it. And you can't visibly see the Lord, but His presence is obvious because of the effect seen in the lives of people who have been touched by His love.

"I really feel a lot better now," Mrs. Daniels told me. "I'm so glad that you decided to come to see me today. Why don't you stay and visit awhile?"

So the three of us, no longer strangers, sat and talked of spiritual things, marveling together at God's amazing grace. Sudden Mrs. Daniels began to sing. "Amazing grace, how sweet the sound that saved a wretch like me." The presence of the Lord filled the room, and Tom and I began to sing the familiar words along with her. "I once was lost, but now I'm found, was blind, but now I see."

Our singing probably would never have won any awards here on earth, but I know that it was pleasing to God. I couldn't actually hear them, but somehow I believe that the angels in heaven were singing along with us.

As I stood up to leave, I turned to Tom and said, "We're having a gathering of believers at our house tonight and I think that the Lord wants you to be there. I just think God has something special planned for you."

Tom didn't hesitate, but answered, "Yes, I believe that He does."

"Eight o'clock," I replied, handing him a card with our address on it.

So at eight o'clock last night, Tom arrived at our house. He looked a bit uncomfortable as he joined the group and took a seat in the far corner of the room. He didn't know many of the songs we were singing, but every now and then I would notice that Tom was singing along with us.

As we continued to lift our voices in praise, the Spirit of God settled upon us as a delicate mist. The presence of the Lord filled the place where we were gathered, and everyone began to sing a new song in the spirit.

Tom dropped suddenly to his knees. "Thank You, Lord! I've been healed. Thank You! Thank You! Lord" Tears streamed down his face. "The pain is gone. It's complete gone. Thank You, Jesus."

Finally when he was able to speak without crying, Tom described the terrible pain he had suffered for the past six months because of thrombosis and phlebitis in both legs. For the past few weeks, Tom had even been unable to work because the problem had become so severe.

"But, tonight Jesus touched me," he declared. "It was like I felt a surge of electricity run through my entire body and now I have no pain at all. I have been healed. I'm sure of it. There is absolutely no pain or swelling."

No human hands had been laid upon Tom. No human lips had mouthed a prayer. Jesus had passed by right in our living room and Tom had reached out to Him in faith. A miracle had happened in our midst.

The things I just related happened yesterday. They didn't happen five years ago, or fifty years ago, or a hundred or even two thousand years ago. These things happened yesterday in a small town in the state of Maryland. And each day throughout the world miracles like this are taking place in the lives of those who dare to believe God. Jesus is alive. He lives. And He is still touching lives today.

CHAPTER 27

AND MANY OTHER THINGS

John wrote in his gospel, *"And there are also many other things which Jesus did, which, if every one of them was written down, I suppose that even the world itself could not contain the books that should be written"* (John 21:25).

And there are also many other things that Jesus has done in my life in the three short years that I have walked with Him. I could go on writing and writing, filling page after page with personal experiences I have had with Jesus Christ. But, this is only the beginning of my spiritual adventure. I am still a young Christian and my walk with the Lord has just really begun. I have no idea of what the future will hold.

Perhaps you have wondered why the title of "Chapter 29" was chosen for this book. If you look at the Book of Acts in your Bible, you will see that it is composed of twenty-eight chapters. There is no "Amen" cited at the conclusion of chapter twenty-eight. Rather, the book remains open-ended, giving the impression that these acts are ongoing and still in progress.

So this book you have read is my own personal chapter in the Book of Acts. I am convinced that every child of God should also be living his or her own chapter that will give testimony to the reality of the Holy Spirit working in and through individual lives

There is nothing unusual about me. I am a Spirit-filled housewife in love with Jesus and spreading the gospel throughout my Jerusalem. The things I have shared in these pages should be the norm in every Christian's life. Expect miracles! Jesus is still seeking ordinary people who will dare to believe that He is the same yesterday, today and forever. He is only hindered by our unbelief.

It is my prayer that this simple little book will inspire you to start believing for miracles in your life. It's time to get out of the boat and walk on the water. Jesus is calling to you right now and saying, "Follow Me."

This book has been written that you might believe that Jesus is the Christ, the Son of the Living God, and that believing, you might have life through His name. God bless you and use you in great and mighty ways.

EPILOGUE
THE YEARS THAT FOLLOWED

The book you have just finished reading has related the adventures of Jean Coleman as a young disciple just learning to walk in the spirit. Over thirty years have passed since she originally put pen to paper and the first edition of "Chapter 29" was published. Since then the testimony of her dramatic life-changing encounter with the Lord Jesus has also been printed in German, Spanish, Norwegian and Telugu and read by thousands of people all around the world.

Who could have guessed what amazing plans the Lord had for this suburban housewife from Maryland as she continued her walk of faith through the years ahead. Do you remember the Thursday night meetings that Jean often mentioned in the book? During the five years that these gatherings were held in the Colemans' home, over a thousand people received Jesus as their Savior and were baptized in the Holy Spirit. Jean's small Bible study, that started with just three women meeting together on a Wednesday morning, quickly attracted forty to fifty women every week.

Jack and Jean began to hold regular monthly meetings on Saturday nights in the high school auditorium that were attended by hundreds of people. "The Family Reunion" reached out across denominational barriers and brought together the family of God for a corporate time of praise, worship and teaching. Anointed preachers from around the world came to share from the Word of God and pray for the sick.

About that same time, Jack became president of the local Full Gospel Business Men's chapter and soon nearly three hundred people were attending the monthly meetings. Jean became an active participant in Women's Aglow Fellowship and served as a worship leader for many years. The Colemans rapidly became sought after speakers at Full Gospel and Aglow meetings up and down the east coast, as well as in churches that were open to the moving of the Spirit.

Jack and Jean were called by God to preach together behind the pulpit in a unique husband and wife ministry that could only be orchestrated by God. They are two people bringing one message in perfect harmony.

Then in 1978 the Colemans again stepped out in faith and founded a charismatic church called The Tabernacle. From the beginning, The Tabernacle was not an ordinary church, but rather a miraculous church that immediately attracted an anointed group of people with unique talents.

As befitting its name, The Tabernacle was always on the move. Meetings were initially held in the local high school, and later moved to a small community hospital. Then, through the miraculous intervention of God, two Jewish business men granted the church use of a 115,000 square foot building that had recently been vacated. Only a year later, The Tabernacle purchased a beautiful eleven-year-old elementary school for one million dollars. Would you believe that the county had a shortage of young children and put the school on the market? It's amazing how God works, isn't it?

With its own permanent building, The Tabernacle continued to grow and soon became the largest church in the city of Laurel, Maryland. Their conferences were attended by hundreds of people from many area churches, and it wasn't long before The Tabernacle became recognized as an International Christian Center.

The Tabernacle began to hold international conferences that attracted pastors and church leaders from all around the world. Because the building was so large, the many delegates to the conferences actually lived in the church for two weeks. The Tabernacle congregation worked day and night to provide all the needs of their guests. Many of the members even took vacations to cook and serve meals, clean bathrooms, help with the meetings, and even do laundry.

Every year at Easter, the Tabernacle sponsored what was advertised as a unique drive-thru experience. Hundreds of cars lined up for blocks waiting their turn to enter the church parking lot where a series of action scenes from the Bible could be viewed. Over a hundred costumed members of The Tabernacle took part in this moving representation of the Easter story and thousands of hearts were touched.

Jack and Jean served as co-pastors of The Tabernacle for twenty years, with their son, John, working with them in the position of associate pastor. As the ministry of The Tabernacle became recognized around the world, the Colemans began to receive invitations to speak internationally. The Lord was honoring Jean's prayer as a young Christian to open the doors for the two of them to go to the nations and minister to millions.

Meanwhile, Jean had become a free lance writer, regularly contributing to some of the nation's leading Christian magazines and began to travel extensively as a conference speaker. Having developed a deep love for pastors' wives, she starting writing a monthly newsletter called "The Pastor's Helpmate" that was mailed to thousands of ministerial wives. Jean also became known throughout the body of Christ as a worship leader and composer of worship choruses, many of which are still being sung around the world today.

Jean's true calling and her greatest anointing is that of a Bible teacher. Her simple child-like faith continues to be in evidence through the parables and simple down to earth illustrations she uses to unlock the mysteries of kingdom living. Her desire is to open the scriptures and make them come alive in the hearts of all who sit under the sound of her voice.

Jack and Jean never went to Bible college or seminary. They have no degrees. But they have taught in Bible colleges all around the world, sat on platforms with Christian leaders from many nations, and spoken in conferences attended by thousands. They have laid hands upon the sick and seen them recover. They have prayed with multitudes to receive Jesus. They are living proof that God uses ordinary people to be His vessels.

In 1998 the Colemans resigned as pastors of The Tabernacle to go into fulltime overseas' ministry and continue their outreach to the far corners of the earth. For the past fifteen years, Jack and Jean have been making several major trips each year, reaching every continent with the gospel. Their hearts have been especially linked together with the nation of India where their church built a school and several orphanages. Jean refers to India as her spiritual home, and together they have preached in literally hundreds of churches and meetings in this predominantly Hindu nation.

Although they minister in many large meetings, Jack and Jean have a real heart for village ministry in undeveloped countries. They have often visited Niger, Africa where they teach in the villages through the telling of stories and simple dramas. They have also ministered extensively throughout the nation of Peru. The list of countries where they have preached the gospel is really too long to include in this brief summary.

Jack and Jean now reside in Knoxville, Tennessee where they are members of a large Spirit-filled church. Jean continues to teach two Bible studies a week, and they also have the oversight of a care group that meets regularly in their home. The Colemans have just purchased the airline tickets for their twenty-first trip to India that is scheduled to take place in January of 2013. God continues to answer their prayer, "Use us, Lord!"

No longer a babe in Christ, Jean Coleman has become a spiritual mother, serving as a role model to Christian women throughout the world. With God, all things are possible. Look at what happened to Jean!